Traveling With Your Grandkids

Virginia Smith Spurlock

AAA PUBLISHING

President & CEO	Robert Darbelnet
Executive Vice President, Publishing & Administration	Rick Rinner
Managing Director, Travel Information	Bob Hopkins
Director, Product Development	Bill Wood
Director, Sales & Marketing	John Coerper
Director, Purchasing & Corporate Services	Becky Barrett
Director, Business Development	Gary Sisco
Director, Tourism Information Development	Michael Petrone
Director, Travel Information	Jeff Zimmerman
Director, Publishing Operations	Susan Sears
Director, GIS/Cartography	Jan Coyne
Director, Publishing/ GIS Systems & Development	Ramin Kalhor
Product Manager	Nancy Jones, CTC
Managing Editor, Product Development	Margaret Cavanaugh
AAA Travel Store & E-Store Manager	Sharon Edwards
Print Buyer	Laura Cox
Manager, Product Support	Linda Indolfi
Manager, Electronic Media Design	Mike McCrary
Manager, Pre-Press & Quality Services	Tim Johnson
Manager, Graphic Communication Services	Yvonne Macklin
Project Coordinator	Sandy Tate
Art Director	Barbra Natali
Cover and Interior Page Design	Joanne McNamara
Paginator	Tony Pomales

ISBN 1-56251-581-0
Stock Number: 144801
Published by AAA Publishing,
1000 AAA Drive, Heathrow, Florida 32746

Printed in the USA by Banta Book Group

Cover Photo Courtesy of © Disney Enterprises, Inc.

ABOUT THE AUTHOR

Virginia Smith Spurlock is a psychologist, author, world-traveler and devoted grandmother of six grandchildren and two great grandchildren. In addition to *Traveling With Your Grandkids*, she has written articles for many publications and co-authored *Cruising Canada by Car. . . Good Times on a Budget*.

Since the death of her husband Charles, she has continued to live and write in Nashville and Clifton, Tenn., and remains an ardent traveler, with and without her grandchildren.

Author Virginia Smith Spurlock may be contacted at: VSSpurlock@cs.com

DEDICATION

To my beloved late husband, my children and children-in-law, without whom there would be no grandchildren, and to my wonderful grandchildren, without whom there would be no book.

ACKNOWLEDGEMENTS

My infinite gratitude to Nancy Jones, whose persistence in locating me brought this book to life.

Special thanks, too, to Rachel and Melvin Bell, Anne and Joe Eaton, Sarah and Bill Roehrig and Elizabeth Massey, who graciously answered my many questions and shared their own wonderful camping experiences with children and grandchildren.

FOREWORD

Being the oldest grandchild, I had the privilege of going on three trips with both Granny and Grandpa. They took turns driving and the non-driver always sat in back with me. Grandpa was not a game player, but he told great stories – lots of times they were about when my Dad and his two brothers and sisters were growing up. I still remember those stories. They were so funny and so real sometimes I thought I was there, too.

During my spring break when I was in the second grade, Granny took me on a cruise to the Caribbean. It was my first cruise and I loved it. In the Dominican Republic, I went snorkeling for the first time. With flippers on my feet, goggles over my eyes and the snorkeling tube in my mouth, I swam in the sea right along- side many varieties of colorful tropical fish. Each time I came out of the water, though, Granny was right there armed with sunblock and suntan lotion. I hated it and complained a lot, but she just smiled and went right on piling it on. Later, though, I thanked her. I didn't come back to the United States with the beautiful tan I had wanted, but at least I didn't have sun poisoning as one boy on our ship did.

– Stephanie

Due to my handicap, I can't talk or write, so my Dad, who accompanies Granny and me on trips, is doing it for me.

Several Christmases ago, Granny took my older sister, Stephanie, and us to Walt Disney World. It was wonderful. I didn't stop smiling the whole week. I loved the rides, the color, the music and having my picture made with Snow White and many of the other Disney characters. Because I am in a wheelchair, we were allowed to enjoy the rides and attractions without waiting in line. Stephanie, Dad and Granny loved that, too. Stephanie even said she didn't ever want to come back there without me.

My favorite ride was "It's a Small World" and I think it was Granny's, too. We rode it a lot. I loved the music and having Granny sit by me, pointing out things and people from faraway countries was great.

– Sarah, with her dad Jeff

My name is Katharine Smith Winstead, but everyone calls me Katie. The Smith part of my name is part of Granny's, too.

When Granny and I go on trips, she always makes me keep a journal. That's OK 'cause I'm going to be a writer when I grow up. She says it's my personal book and nobody can read it unless I say it's OK. So far, I haven't let anybody see it.

I was so excited when Granny said the people at AAA wanted us grandchildren to write the foreword to her book. I'm not sure what a foreword is, but I asked her if it would be published and she said, "Yes." I'm 9 years old and already I'm published!

– Katie

I like to go on trips with Granny. The only thing I don't like is she likes to drive and it takes so long to get anywhere. I like to fly. I've only flown once. That was the time Granny took the whole family on a Christmas cruise. I heard Granny say we were landing in Miami and I thought it was her "ami" until I heard my Mom call it "Miami", too. I was confused and I asked them whose "ami" it was. They laughed and said it was the name of a city. I was only 3 then. I know better now. This summer we are going to Washington, D.C. My sister Katie is going, too. We were going to Space Camp, but after seeing so much about Washington on TV, we really wanted to go there, so we are. The sad part is we're going to drive. I asked Granny if we could fly, but she said there were so many things to see and do on the way and we'd miss them if were flew. I guess it'll be all right.

– John

Last summer when I was 4, I got to go on my first trip alone with Granny. We went to Chattanooga, Tenn., to the big aquarium and the creative museum. I especially liked the museum. I got to go on a pretend archaeological dig and look for dinosaur bones and other fossils. When we left the museum we were hungry and Granny was looking around for a restaurant. "Let's go to the Burger King™." I said. She said she didn't think there was one anywhere nearby and maybe we should try Friday's®. But I told her I knew where there was a Burger King and I was right. It was straight across the street from us.

I like to go with Granny and, besides, she needs me to help her find things.

– William

TABLE OF CONTENTS

INTRODUCTION

If you are a grandparent in the 55-plus age group – and you probably are if you're reading this book – you may be surprised to know that there are about 60 million of us in the United States today.

We are healthier. We are living longer. We are (or want to be) very involved in our grandchildren's lives. We're wealthier and able to spend more on the grandkids than ever. But we don't want to spoil them. We want to get to know them and let them get to know us and our values and ideals.

What's a good way to establish a close relationship with your children's children? By relaxing and having fun with them on a trip, of course.

Intergenerational travel is up. With more and more grandparents taking kids on a vacation, hotels, cruise ships, tour groups, dude ranches, even some museums and art galleries are offering more kid-friendly activities and grandparent discounts. I see this as increasing greatly over the next few years as our numbers increase. It is estimated that we will be 72 million strong in five years and 80 million in 10 years.

Where you want to travel with your grandchildren depends on their ages, interests and maturity levels, to say nothing of your own interests and budget. All kids are different. Keep in mind that children ages 4-7 have limited attention spans and need lots of hands-on activities. Building sandcastles and chasing the waves at the beach may be ideal.

Teenagers bore so easily that they need their own input into whatever is planned. A budding artist, young thespian, music lover or dance enthusiast might revel in that smorgasbord of culture – New York City. Those 8-12 years old are the easiest to please generally and like a great diversity of activities. Sightseeing to them is not a dirty word. They may love historical Virginia or Boston, and astronaut wannabes adore the space centers in Florida or Alabama.

So assuming you aren't nearly ready for a rocking chair, are gung-ho to hit the road and genuinely love being with your grandchildren, you're probably an ideal candidate for this great adventure. Remember though: When taking grandchildren on vacation, there's more involved than simply packing a suitcase, picking up the kids and hopping in the car. It takes a great deal of planning and preparation to make any trip special . . . and that's especially true of intergenerational vacations.

I hope this book will make things easier and pave the way for many wonderful trips.

Shortly before my husband's death, our 7-year-old granddaughter Stephanie expressed a fervent desire to see the White House. We promised to take her there during her next summer vacation. When I was suddenly widowed, I asked myself if I were brave enough to undertake such a venture alone. No question that she wanted to go and so did I but . . .

I discussed it with my son and his ex-wife. Without hesitation, each gave me a fervent "go ahead." That boosted my self-confidence. The first thing I did was buy a cellular phone for the car in case of an emergency. Then I sat down with Stephanie to pore over maps and travel books.

Our week in Washington, D.C., was fantastic. Since then I have become totally addicted to traveling with my grandchildren . . . and they are equally enthusiastic. We have toured, cruised, shared experiences unique to us and, in so doing, established close, long-term relationships.

CHAPTER 1

GET READY

S tart by getting the go-ahead from the parents. This must be done even before mentioning the possibility of a trip to your grandchild. In case one or both parents give a thumbs down to the idea, they won't look like bad guys in the eyes of their child. Let's say, for example, that there isn't a definite no, but you sense reticence on the part of one or both parents to allow their child to be carried away on an adventure over which they will have little control. Go easy. No hurt feelings, no pouting. Keep a smile on your face and let it drop, at least for the time being. It will soon be time to put plan B into action.

Plan B is to invite the reticent parent and your grandchild on a day's outing. Do something you think both parent and child - but especially parent - will particularly enjoy. You plan it, you execute it and you pay for it. If it's a memorable day, then some time later, ease the intergenerational vacation idea into the conversation again and reassess the reaction. If their reaction is still negative, I suggest you forget it and satisfy yourself with one-day excursions with your grandchild - at least for the time being.

Assuming the scenario doesn't happen or your plan B does the trick, you now have the sanction of Mom and Dad. Great! But you may have to make some tough decisions. The first one is probably the most important.

HOW OLD IS OLD ENOUGH?

Of course, your decision depends on the maturity of the individual child. But you'll probably find, as we did, that a minimum age of 4 is a good guideline. Along with that rule comes a promise to the younger ones that their time will come. Special day excursions or overnights at Granny and Grandpa's house can be planned for the small fry left behind.

A situation may arise when there is a grandchild who won't want to go and who, regardless of chronological age, isn't ready to leave Mom, Dad and home. Fine. Be sure to remember that grandchild with something special if you travel with a brother, sister or cousin. Chances are the child will be ready next year.

On the other hand, there may be a child who *you* know isn't ready (even if he and his parents think he is). In this case, the overnight trial run discussed later in this chapter is even more essential. Try to be as objective as possible when assessing your chances of success on a longer vacation. Miracles happen and a child who seems hopelessly unprepared for a long trip away may turn out to be the best traveling companion ever. But if homesickness is a possibility, the child probably won't be able to handle the trip - now. It's kinder to promise another try next year - and a lovely gift when you return from your trip - to ease the disappointment.

SHOULD YOU TAKE ONE GRANDCHILD OR TWO?

Next decision. If you have more than one grandchild, you must decide whether to take one, two or more of them. Because, chances are, when a trip is mentioned, all of your grandchildren from age 2 and up will line up to go. Obviously, you'll give them all a turn in a way that's fair and appropriate. I don't have to tell you how to do that. You love them all and you'll make sure they're OK about who goes and when. But the guidelines we've developed over the years will help you decide how many to take on each vacation.

Taking one grandchild at a time is unquestionably the easiest and most desirable option. Nothing can replace that one-on-one relationship, especially during a child's early years. So, if at all possible, travel with one grandchild.

Taking one grandchild at a time is unquestionably

the easiest and most desirable option.

Nothing can replace that one-on-one relationship,

especially during a child's early years.

So, if at all possible, travel with one grandchild.

If you have several grandchildren, you can still enjoy traveling with them. You just have to do a little more planning. You can keep the peace by dividing your vacation time into smaller segments, maybe keeping one vacation just for *you*. Taking one child on each trip will make everybody happy and allow you to give and receive that all-important individual attention.

If this utopian arrangement doesn't work for you, here are more guidelines to help.

When there are two grandparents, and two children of compatible ages (ages 4-7 or 8-11 or 12-16) and interests, each grandparent can spend special time with each grandchild. My husband and I traveled quite a bit with more than one of our grandchildren, and we found great joy in seeing things, both familiar and new, come alive through their young eyes. When two grandchildren are with you, there's also the advantage of their playing together, which leaves you with a little rest and relaxation time.

With a partner, you might even consider three children - but no more than four - unless you opt for the more expensive cruise or dude ranch vacation where you may take as many as you can afford or tolerate. Cruises or dude ranches that cater to children offer a variety of activities for different ages. They also are the easiest, most convenient way to accommodate everybody. Yes, you will lose out on the one-on-one time, but you'll still have the children all to yourself - without their parents - and that makes it special. Actually, a trip of this kind can be a lot of fun for everybody, which is what a vacation is all about, isn't it? Check out Chapter 12 for information about cruise and ranch vacations with children.

If you are a single grandparent, as I am now, or if you're traveling without a spouse, do not plan to take more than two children at a time.

You may find that preteens or teenagers want a companion such as a sibling, cousin or friend of comparable age to accompany you. Be as sure as you can that they are compatible. That doesn't mean that they won't argue or even fight.

If this does happen, it's important that you remain objective. Stay out of their disagreements unless it endangers life or limb. Ordinarily, they will settle these things quickly if left to themselves. This age group will need and want to help in the pretrip planning. I allow each to set three priorities - things they really want to see and do at our chosen destination - and promise at least one, or more if possible.

The slightly younger age group (ages 8-10) are probably not going to be as aware of things to do and places to go, so you and their parents (if they live a distance away from you) will need to help them research the area and then make their top choices. Your younger grandchildren will likely be happy just to pack a suitcase and go. Even though you tell them what to expect, you will need to repeat this each day. Attention spans for this group are limited.

TAKE IT ONE STEP AT A TIME

For you grandparents who live some distance from your grandchildren and haven't had the chance to establish and maintain a good rapport with them, start simple and go easy. Visit the family for a few days before making your decision about the vacation. Become familiar with their lifestyles, schedules, their likes and dislikes. Get to know them and let them know you before you launch into an elaborate, long trip.

The Overnight Trial Run

If your grandchild is not yet 8 - and, again, I don't recommend vacationing with any under the age of 4 without their parents - you may want to take a local overnight trial run. I suggest local because you can easily contact mom and dad if the child becomes unhappy in the middle of the night. Plan some in-town activities for a couple of days, then arrange a sleepover at a motel or hotel.

Remember to keep your plans flexible and easy.

This is getting-to-know-you time, a chance to

determine the dynamics between you and

your youngster, an opportunity to get a

feel for what it will be like to take

a longer trip together.

Depending on the child's age, you may want to visit a museum or take them to the zoo. Perhaps there's a children's theater or a good movie playing. Allow plenty of swim time in the hotel swimming pool before dinner. Let your grandchild help decide where to eat, whether it's the hotel restaurant or perhaps a favorite spot nearby where he seldom goes. It could be even be a pizza delivered to your room and enjoyed while watching a favorite TV program. The next morning, a room-service breakfast and leisurely swim before checkout time can be the perfect ending to this mini-vacation.

Remember to keep your plans flexible and easy. This is getting-to-know-you time, a chance to determine the dynamics between you and your youngster, an opportunity to get a feel for what it will be like to take a longer trip together.

When your time together is over, be sure to consult your grandchild as to whether he still wants to go away without his parents. Even if he was eager to go when you talked about it earlier, this trial run may be enough for him for now. A friend of mine recently took her 4-year-old granddaughter to a theme park with less than happy results. "It was a disaster," she reported. "Stacy wanted her mother. Nothing pleased her. I doubt that I'll try that again."

If you feel that your trial vacation was not as successful as you had hoped, don't be discouraged. It could be a situation like my friend's when the child is simply not ready for vacationing away from Mom and Dad. Or you may find that *you* are not ready to assume that responsibility. Chronological age is not a true measure of emotional development on either end of the spectrum. You may want to try again in a year or so or when the parents feel their youngster is ready. If it is you who feel you aren't suited to traveling with little ones anymore, explain to the child and the parents that you believe shorter-term activities will be better.

If all went well on your mini-vacation and everyone decides on a longer one, four to five days will probably be long enough for your first vacation, especially if your grandchild is younger than 8.

Where to Go, What to Do
Deciding where to go and what to do depends on the child and, perhaps more important, the child's age. If your grandchild is in the 4-6 range, you may want to opt for the beach or perhaps the mountains. If you're wondering what you'd do with young kids at the beach when it rains for five days straight, you'll find that subject covered in Chapter 15 Homesickness and Other Problems.

Sightseeing is not high on a young child's priority list. Check with your travel agent about hotels that have planned activities for children. After all, you may need a little private time, too. Keep your driving time to a minimum. Long driving days require even more patience, planning and preparation.

Children of today -

especially smart grandchildren like yours

and mine - are worldly and knowledgeable.

Even young ones know what they want to see and

do. If their goal is realistic and you can live with

it, try to make that the focus of the trip.

It won't be hard to find out what your grandchild wants to do. Children of today - especially smart grandchildren like yours and mine - are worldly and knowledgeable. Even young ones know what they want to see and do. If their goal is realistic and you can live with it, try to make that the focus of the trip.

Whether the activity is making a sandcastle on the beach, checking out Plymouth Rock or petting a dolphin at SeaWorld®, it deserves top priority. Remember, though, that *you* have the last word. Consider your own interests. Do not - I repeat, do not - attempt any type of activity that you do not feel up to physically, emotionally or financially.

Hiking the Appalachian Trail from Georgia to Maine would tax my physical capabilities, as would white-water rafting down the Snake River. A week in Paris would strain my budget and I intensely dislike fishing. So I eliminate these activities early in the planning stage. Additionally, I ordinarily do not take my grandchildren to amusement or theme parks. I think these are more fun for immediate families and it isn't my intention to replace such vacations but to supplement them with a different kind that's enjoyable for grandchildren and grandparents alike.

With your destination mutually decided upon, you and your grandchild should visit the public library and check out books relating to the area of the country that you plan to visit. If you live in different parts of the country, ask your grandchild's parents to help her with the trip research. Then you and your grandchild can have telephone meetings to set priorities.

Your local AAA office can furnish you with road maps, TourBook® guides, brochures and general information about your destination. AAA can make travel arrangements and hotel reservations as well. If you're a member of AAA, you can call the exclusive phone number (866) AAA-SAVE to obtain the lowest rates with AAA partners. AAA also can help plan your route in a TripTik® routing, if you wish.

Don't forget to ask about discounts for seniors. Frequently hotel or motel chains offer discounts and allow children to stay and eat free when traveling with parents or grandparents. And you may receive a discount on your hotel or motel room if you're a member of AAA or another auto club or association. Be sure to ask when you make your reservations, whether you call or your travel agent does it for you. Don't hesitate to ask for the best deal for you. Some of the larger hotel chains, such as the Hilton with its Hilton HHonors program, have special senior packages with up to 50 percent off room rates. These hotels often offer specials for grandchildren, too. Check with your favorite hotel chain.

Poring over the materials and planning the things you want to do - even over the telephone - is great fun for you and your grandchild. The anticipation is almost as good as being there.

Next on Your Agenda

How to get there is next on your planning agenda. If your destination is a great distance away, you may want to fly into the nearest city and rent a car for visiting outlying areas. Airplane travel is always exciting, but long trips by air, as well as on the ground, can be tedious and boring if there's no advance planning. Crayons, coloring books, reading material and handheld electronic games are easy to carry onboard and fun to use.

Be sure to carry some chewing gum to chew during take-offs and landings. It helps keep the sometimes-painful pressure from building in children's ears.

Traveling by car is my favorite way to go. Our country is so beautiful and there are such fascinating things to see and experience every few miles. It's amazing how even the youngest child will notice the changes in topography as you drive along. The trip will lend itself to great conversations and storytelling. Keep your plans flexible enough to allow stops for anything you or your grandchild may want to see.

With only one grandparent-driver-entertainer, you may want to stop for a break every couple of hours to allow both of you to relax, move about a little and perhaps have a snack before driving on. If there are two drivers, plan to switch about every one-and-a-half to two hours. This way each grandparent can play games with the grandchild while the other drives.

Inexpensive travel games are available at stores where toys are sold. One popular game is *Where in the World is Carmen San Diego?* Another is Milton Bradley's *Memory.* Take your grandchild with you when you shop and he certainly will tell you what interests him. Studying the map and plotting your course is also fun, as is reading aloud from the child's favorite books or from books about the places you're going to visit.

You may want to make up your own games or play those that interested your children when they were growing up.

Storytelling, though, is probably the favorite of all youngsters, regardless of their age, and is marvelous for grandparent couples or singles. "Tell me about my Dad when he was little. . . . How did Uncle Chuck fall out of the tree and break his arm? . . . Were you in a real war, Grandpa?" These and a million other questions could keep you and your grandchild talking all the way from North Carolina to California.

You can turn the tables, too. Let him tell you a favorite story or ask him about his friends, favorite things and fun times. After all, getting to know each other better is a key part of this trip, and the relationship you build now is the groundwork for open communication later, during those difficult teen years when it often seems nobody talks or listens to anybody.

Be Prepared

As with any trip, be prepared. Prudence dictated my buying a cellular phone before starting out for Washington with my granddaughter. It came in very handy when we had a flat tire on the interstate. AAA was there shortly and we were on our way quickly. I strongly recommend that you carry a portable phone when on your trip. That way you can relax and know contact with an auto club or someone else can be quickly made should an emergency arise.

Your itinerary should be flexible. The weather may be totally uncooperative. Or that eagerly anticipated activity could prove disappointing. If you or your grandchild becomes tired and irritable, cancel your afternoon plans and take a long, cool dip in the hotel pool. If it's raining, go to the movies or see what the movie selections are on your hotel room television. The main thing is to never feel that any plan is etched in stone. If one thing doesn't work out, there's always another activity. After all, a vacation is for spontaneity and fun!

Is There an Easier Way?

Isn't there an easier way to enjoy a few days with my grandchild? Sure there is. Maybe a freewheeling kind of vacation isn't for you. Maybe you aren't comfortable driving long distances, flying into strange cities, renting cars or making reservations. You love your grandchildren, though, and you would like to show and share with them the world in which we live.

Don't despair. There are tour companies to help you accomplish similar goals without the planning, driving and other stressful activities.

Contact your local AAA office. The AAA travel agent can give you information about special grandparent programs at Walt Disney World and other destinations.

Disney Cruise Line has a variety of special family packages, combining a cruise with a visit to the Walt Disney World® Resort. Call your travel agent to learn more about these packages.

Elderhostel, Inc. now has a variety of intergenerational programs for grandparents and grandchildren. The folks there can be contacted by writing them at 11 Ave. de Lafayette, Boston, MA 02111, or by calling toll-free (877) 426-8056.

> ❝ Never feel that any plan is etched in stone. If one thing doesn't work out, there's always another activity. After all, a vacation is for spontaneity and fun! ❞

CHAPTER 2

GET SET

D eparture time is approaching. Excitement is running high. It's time to pack and - even more importantly - it's time to make and agree on rules and expectations. No matter where you're going or how you're getting there, whether by car, plane, bus or burro, one essential thing to remember is: Pack light.

This is not always easy to do but absolutely necessary for intergenerational travel. Neither you nor your grandchild should do any undue lifting or carrying. A suitcase on wheels for you and a backpack for your grandchild plus a shared tote will be ideal.

Packing doesn't have to be a nightmare. A simple tip is: If you question whether you need something, leave it at home. Make a list of what to bring and stick to it

Things to remember:

- ✔ You don't need a million pairs of underwear and socks; they can be washed and hung in the bathroom at night.

- ✔ Bring clothing that can be mixed and matched.

- ✔ Darker colors don't show dirt as easily.

- ✔ Blue jeans and shorts (according to the weather) are excellent choices for boys or girls.

- ✔ Include extra T-shirts for emergencies.

✔ Take one semi-dressed-up outfit in case you go to the theater or a nicer restaurant.

✔ A light jacket, preferably with a hood, or sweater is necessary for cool evenings.

✔ Don't forget your toothbrush, sleepwear, swimsuit and cover-up and a favorite toy.

You and your grandchild should pack together with parental suggestions, of course. This way you won't be hearing "Where's my toothbrush?" or "I can't find my socks" every day.

Taking luggage your grandchild packed herself (with a lot of help, of course) gives her a feeling of independence and teaches organization. Let her know she is responsible for her own things, including repacking, when it's time to change locations.

Taking luggage your grandchild packed herself (with a lot of help, of course) gives her a feeling of independence and teaches organization. Let her know she is responsible for her own things, including repacking, when it's time to change locations.

In your jointly used tote bag, you might want to pack things you'll share, such as a hair dryer, travel clock, shampoo, toothpaste and a fever thermometer. I also include our journals, scrapbook, a small tape recorder and tapes for the child too young to write. I require the kids keep a journal. It's like a private diary and need never be shared unless the author so chooses. Writing in our journals is an every-night, just-before-sleep ritual for my grandchild and me. When we're too tired, we do it the next morning before starting out. No exceptions.

If your grandchild has daily medications, keep them in a separate compartment of your suitcase. Ask the parents to write out the correct dosage and keep a running record of when and how much you administer.

You also should have a copy of the parent's medical insurance card. These are documents that grandparents should have on hand any time they're in temporary custody of their grand-children, regardless of location.

One vitally important item to have in your

possession is a parental statement, signed by

both parents and notarized, giving you permission

to travel with your grandchild and allowing you to give

permission for emergency medical treatment

in case of accident or illness.

One vitally important item to have in your possession is a parental statement, signed by both parents and notarized, giving you permission to travel with your grandchild and allowing you to give permission for emergency medical treatment in case of accident or illness.

Whether you're traveling out of the United States or not, the best kind of identification you can have is your passport. Canada, Mexico and the islands of the Caribbean do not require passports for native-born citizens, but you must have valid identification such as a driver's license and voter registration card. If your grandchild does not have a passport, carry his birth certificate and a recent photo ID and the parental permission statement.

SETTING LIMITS, MAKING RULES

Who makes the rules? You do. Set aside some time before you leave to sit down with your grandchild and his parents and outline your expectations of the child and the rules he will have to follow. No vacation adventure should begin without such an understanding. It is doubtful that you will have discipline problems if you and your grandchild are clear about limits. This doesn't have to be a deadly serious or heavy-handed discussion, just a friendly, clarifying talk so everybody knows what to expect from each other during your vacation.

It needs to be understood up front that it is you who always has the last word. When you say no, it is definitely no and is not negotiable. Undoubtedly, during your time together, your grandchild will test the limits. But if you're consistent and never say no if you mean maybe, the child will stop testing you.

First, it needs to be understood up front that it is you who always has the last word. When you say no, it is definitely no and is not negotiable. Undoubtedly, during your time together, your grandchild will test the limits. But if you're consistent and never say no if you mean maybe, the child will stop testing you.

My cellular phone is only for emergencies, and this is something I emphasize early on during each trip - although my granddaughters especially find it a great temptation to use the phone. Both are prone to ask to *see* it on occasions and when asked why, their response is always the same. "It's an emergency. I need to call my friends and tell them where I am."

Parents need to be involved when you're establishing the rules for your trip. You don't want to allow your grandchild to do things that are strict no-nos at home. Also, they need to answer some important questions. Of course, you might ask the child, but then the answers might be a tad self-serving. For example, you'll want to know:

✔ When is bedtime? Is this flexible and, if so, how flexible?

✔ Are there daily routines that need to be strictly adhered to?

✔ Are there any allergies - food or other kinds - to watch out for?

✔ How much spending money will the child have and how much can he depend on you to supplement?

✔ Does he swim? Does he dive? Is he allowed in the deep end of the pool? Does he use earplugs when swimming? A nose guard? What kind of sunscreen does he use?

You and your grandchild also need to understand and agree on certain other things before you go. Very likely, both of you have established customs and habits, things you really want to do each day. Now is the time to spell them out. For example, 4-year-old Katie always wanted to sleep with her tattered baby blanket. She told me about this and I saw to it that the blanket was packed first thing each day we traveled. Grandma, on the other hand, wanted to take a 20-minute siesta every afternoon. We worked that out, too. Katie turned the TV on low and watched cartoons while her grandmother snoozed . . . and woke refreshed and ready for new adventures.

Let your grandchild know that plans might have to change sometimes . . . and that, if they do, the two of you will make new plans together. She should know that some things both of you would like to do might be beyond your endurance or budget. Let her know that if you can't do something, you will discuss the reasons honestly, but, when these decisions are made, they are final.

CHAPTER 3

Go!

Departure day is finally here. The car is packed and the gas tank is filled. You've checked 20 times and are finally sure you have all the necessary items: cash, credit cards, travelers checks, parental permission, identification for both of you, glasses, sunglasses, tissues, wet wipes, your senior discount cards, reservation details, confirmations and any personal items you absolutely need.

You have explained to your grandchild that, because you love him and want him to be safe, his seat is in the back. If your grandchild is under the age of 1, he should be in a rear-facing infant seat. If your grandchild is between the ages of 1-4, he should be in a forward-facing child safety seat. Children older than 4 should have an appropriate restraint to help the lap and shoulder belts fit better. And it is your rule that he is buckled up. For more information about child safety when traveling, contact your local AAA club or local law enforcement agency. You have a box or carry-on bag (if flying) of electronic and manual travel games, crayons, coloring books, books to read and a favorite toy. My granddaughter Dianne always takes a somewhat road-weary doll that, without a whimper, has been buried in the sand, hung out to dry on a 12th-floor balcony, and dragged off and on a lot of airplanes.

While you're traveling - especially by car - it's a good idea to have a camera close by to capture a fleeting scene you'll want to remember. If you choose not to allow your grandchild to use your camera, I suggest you make one available for her to use. Children see things in different ways from adults and what's important to your grandchild may not be significant to you. Let her take pictures of what appeals to her. At the very least, she'll get a good laugh out of them someday.

My granddaughter Dianne always takes a somewhat

road-weary doll that, without a whimper, has been buried

in the sand, hung out to dry on a 12th-floor balcony,

and dragged off and on a lot of airplanes.

There are many easy-to-use, inexpensive cameras on the market. Disposable cameras are easy to operate and reasonably priced. In addition, camera and filmmakers offer how-to books on photography - even for young children. The photographic industry knows that the earlier kids learn to take pictures, the more likely they are to continue this hobby into adult life. A little camera and a how-to-take-pictures book might make a good Christmas or birthday gift before your trip. Or a delightful "Happy Vacation" present to kick off your travels.

My 6-year-old grandson Jeff, while visiting the U.S. Space and Rocket Center in Huntsville, Ala., took Polaroid shots of the other tourists seated at an outdoor restaurant and presented his pictures to his subjects. Several parents were so enchanted that they took his name and address and wrote to him after they were home. One youngster even became his first-grade pen pal.

Returning from his first granny-grandson trip, John couldn't wait to show off his souvenirs - a T-shirt from Rock City, a plastic whale from an aquarium and some pebbles from the bank of a lake.

"And now, these are for everybody. You're going to love them," he said, beaming with pride as he pulled out the 12

Polaroid pictures he had taken - all of our motel lobby: a chair, a lamp, the chandelier and the ceiling.

In order to preserve your grandchild's own pictures, he needs a scrapbook. These are easy to find and usually inexpensive. Let him choose one that appeals to him. This keepsake can also hold ticket stubs, autographs, picture postcards or anything else he may accumulate along the way.

If your youngster has a camera, a journal and a scrapbook, he really shouldn't need other souvenirs. But whenever did a child resist a gift shop? It's essential for him to know how much he can spend and to understand that, when that money is spent, there is no more. Grandparents should resist becoming bottomless wells of cash for trinkets.

The first question out of your grandchild's mouth is, "How much farther is it?" Then, "Will our hotel pool have a curvy slide?" If you don't feel your balloon of happiness deflate just a little, you are a saint.

My sister and her husband emphasized this strongly to their grandson before leaving for a trip across the country. But on the first night out, 7-year-old Bryan visited the gift shop and came out with several treasures and a dollar left. They were to be gone three weeks and planned to visit places like Disneyland® and Six Flags®. Too bad, Bryan. The wise grandparents stuck to their guns and, even though it was a hard lesson for all of them, there was a good result. The former spendthrift was so eager to share his misadventure with his younger cousin that he made an indelible impression. Cousin William, on his first grandparent-grandchild trip, was so struck with Bryan's sad story that he did a lot of looking and almost no buying in the gift shops. "I don't want to be like poor Bry," he often said. And he came home with only a few dollars less than he had when he left.

At last, you're on your way. Goodbye kisses have been thrown. Seat belts are fastened and you're headed to the interstate. You've just started your monologue on what glorious sights you'll see today and how much fun you're going to have when . . . The first question out of your grandchild's mouth is, "How much farther is it?" Then, "Will our hotel pool have a curvy slide?" If you don't feel your balloon of happiness deflate just a little, you are a saint.

GREAT EXPECTATIONS

Keep your expectations reasonable and you won't be disappointed. Great expectations can mean great disappointment. Your idea of what's fun and meaningful to do on a vacation and your grandchild's idea will probably not be the same. Probably not even close.

For example: On what seemed an especially endless drive across Kansas with my grandson, I spotted a sign advertising an Native American burial ground a few miles away. We quickly decided to go, veered off the highway and drove down some dusty back roads. We finally came to an isolated farmhouse with a paved parking lot, empty except for a few Rhode Island Red chickens pecking the dry earth. We got out of the car and took a rather perfunctory look around. It was obvious that Chuck was not in the least bit interested in this archaeological find. When we got back to the parking lot, though, he had a great time chasing the chickens. Now when anyone mentions Kansas, he quips, "Oh, yeah, that's where those scaredy-cat chickens were."

After returning from a trip through the Great Smoky Mountains with her grandson, my cousin Julie moaned, "I thought John would love hiking to the top of Clingmans Dome. I did when I was his age. But all he talks about are the great peach pancakes we had in Gatlinburg."

On a flight back from Florida one summer vacation, Stephanie and I were upgraded to first class. I was pleased and thought she would be thrilled. But when her father met us at the airport and I told him of our good fortune, he asked her what she thought of first class. "I think it's grossly overrated," she said. "The only thing different was the wash cloths they gave us to wipe our hands on were warm. Big deal."

When we returned from Washington, D.C., you would have thought the only thing Stephanie saw was the pair of ruby-red slippers Judy Garland wore in *The Wizard of Oz* on display at The Smithsonian Institution. Months later, however, when she and her friend were watching the burial of Jacqueline Kennedy Onassis on television, Stephanie's mother heard her explaining about the eternal flame at President John F. Kennedy's grave.

The education your grandchild is getting from your travel experiences together is not always immediately obvious. But it happens, regardless of the short-term memory lapses. So, relax, go with the flow and remember: Kids aren't interested in how educational something is or how much *you* enjoyed it as a child. They just want to have fun. And what's wrong with that?

BE PATIENT

Keep in mind that any family get-together requires patience, particularly when it's the young and not-so-young who are getting together. Remember to really listen and love each other. This vacation can prove to be such a precious time. Going the extra mile is well worth it. The memories you will make are forever.

Now, here the two of you are sitting in the car, journeying down the road to your destination, and your grandchild has just asked you that question signifying impending boredom. This might be the time to play a tape of your grandchild's favorite music or story. A friend of mine tapes fairy tales to play for her grandchildren when they're in the car, whether they're going across town to ballet lessons or to a nearby mall. I've found this works well on longer trips, too.

If there are two grandparents on the trip, the passenger might get into the back seat and play a game or two with the child. You should be well equipped with the recommended travel box. Let your grandchild select what she wants to do. Whether it's a card game, puppet show, reading aloud or playing a board game like Travel Monopoly, it should keep you and your youngster occupied for some time.

A friend of mine tapes fairy tales to play for her grandchildren when they're in the car, whether they're going across town to ballet lessons or to a nearby mall. I've found this works well on longer trips, too.

By the time you begin to tire of this, it'll be time for you to take the wheel and the other grandparent to take over in the back seat. If it's grandfather's turn, he may want to make up his own story; grandfathers are universally good storytellers.

The rest of this book gives overviews of trips to take and places to visit with your grandchildren. The following chapters are not intended to include a complete list of good places to travel with grandchildren, which is almost anyplace you both like, but simply suggestions I hope will inspire you and which you can adapt according to your own interests and time. I give my experiences and opinions about the appropriate ages for grandchildren to enjoy each destination, but *you* are the best judge of your youngster's interest and maturity level. Some kids will adore a city at a far younger age than others. Other may hate a state park even though they're the right age.

The destinations cover a range of possibilities such as parks, cities, states and an entire geographic area. I hope you'll read them all. One or two places just might appeal to you and may turn out to be the perfect vacation for you and your small, beloved guest. Most of all, wherever you choose to go with your grandchild, have fun!

CHAPTER 4

BOSTON AND THE NORTHEAST

B oston is a destination that's appropriate for boys and girls ages 10 and older. When you go for a visit to Boston, don't rent a car. This wonderful, exciting, historic cradle of liberty is, in my opinion, the worst city in America in which to drive. Take an airport limousine to your hotel and tour from there. You and your grandchild will be safer and happier. Don't worry about getting around. There are great trolley tours available and the MBTA subway system is excellent.

For this trip, perhaps more than most because of its historic significance, you need to prepare your youngster a little bit. Some suggested books and poems you may want to read together are:

✔ *Paul Revere's Ride* by Henry Wadsworth Longfellow

✔ *Boston's Freedom Trail* by Terry Dunnahoo

✔ *The Bells of Freedom* by Dorothy Gilman

✔ *The Drums of April* by Charles Mergendahl

In Boston, select a hotel near the Prudential Center. This central area is a pick-up point for most of the trolleys. For your first adventure in this old city, you need to take the famous Boston Duck Tours. It leaves the Prudential Center every half hour from 9 a.m. until an hour before sunset from April through November. Because it's so popular, it frequently sells out before noon. Tickets may be purchased up to two days in advance.

"No way!" My 11-year-old grandson John complained when told how early we would have to get up. "All these historical things have been here for hundreds of years. They'll wait."

"They will," I replied, "but the Ducks won't." The Ducks are authentic, renovated World War II amphibious landing vehicles that take you on a journey on the Charles River. While on the ride, a tour guide will tell you little-known stories of places that made Boston the birthplace of freedom. Soon after you begin the ride, the vehicle suddenly splashes down into the river. This half-boat-half-bus takes you on a cruise downriver under the Longfellow Bridge and back for an unbelievable waterside view of Boston. Even my sometimes hard-to-please grandson John was impressed by this.

I recommend that you take this tour on your first day because, not only is it great fun, it also gives you an overview of what there is for you and your grandchild to go see and visit. Unlike the trolleys, you can't get on and off whenever you choose.

Before you go to your hotel room, stop by the concierge desk and ask for brochures of the Beantown Trolley and find out where the nearest passenger pick-up is. Tickets probably will be available there at a discount. These trolleys run all day long and stop at 19 different places of interest, including the Museum of Fine Arts and the USS *Constitution* in Charlestown. You may get off and on as many times during the day as you wish at no extra charge. If you study the map in the brochure carefully, the two of you should be able to plan a day-by-day itinerary that will please both generations.

CREATE YOUR OWN LIST

Here is some information about a few of the places that John and I particularly enjoyed. You will, of course, create your own list.

The Paul Revere House is the oldest home in downtown Boston. Nearby is the Old North Church, where the two lanterns were hung on April 18, 1775, signifying to Paul Revere that the Redcoats were on their way to Concord by sea. Be sure to read Longfellow's poem before you visit these sites. Paul Revere, John Hancock, Robert Trent Paine, Samuel Adams and Elizabeth Foster "Mother" Goose are buried in the Granary Burying Ground on Tremont Street.

The USS *Constitution* Museum - where visitors may load a cannon, steer a squarerigger at sea and command *Old Ironsides* in battle by using computer technology - is a must, especially for the small set. Next door is the Bunker Hill Pavilion where the Battle of Bunker Hill is presented in a surround-sound amphitheater.

Boston by Little Feet is a special hour-long volunteer-guided walking tour for children ages 6-12. Call (617) 367-2345 for more information.

Don't miss the New England Aquarium, a fabulous aquatic zoo where more than 50 exhibits feature sea turtles, eels, sharks and a variety of other fish swimming in what looks like a natural habitat. We especially loved the strutting penguins that inhabit a large salt-water tray at the base of a tank. The aquarium also has whale-watching cruises that take you through the harbor and out to sea.

For a fun time, visit the Boston Tea Party Ship and Museum, where history comes alive. You and your grandchild may participate with Colonial guides in the reenactment of the original tea party and toss chests of tea overboard.

The Children's' Museum at 300 Congress Street contains four floors of fun for kids through age 10. There's a giant maze to climb and an exhibit called Build It Construction Zone! that features a construction site filled with building materials for hands-on activity. Plus your youngsters could find themselves acting on TV. Young computer whizzes will love the Computer Museum. The exhibits are hands-on and easy to use. The gift shop is unique, too.

❝ For a fun time, visit the Boston Tea Party Ship and Museum, where history comes alive. You and your grandchild may participate with Colonial guides in the reenactment of the original tea party and toss chests of tea overboard. ❞

Sports enthusiasts shouldn't miss the Sports Museum of New England - Fleet Center. It covers 22 different sports from the high school level to pro sports. My grandson came away from here poorer - but happy. The museum shop is like a sports gallery with everything collectors desire.

While you're in the sports mood, don't forget to check Major League Baseball's Boston Red Sox schedule of games at Fenway Park. They play plenty of home games during the summer months. The number to call is (617) 267-1700. If there isn't a home game, you might like a behind-the-scenes tour of the park. Tours are conducted from 10 to 1 Monday through Friday.

The age and interests of your grandchild will undoubtedly dictate the side trips you'll want to take near Boston. Check with Brush Hill Tours, which is a sister to the Beantown Trolleys, about their daily bus trips.

When it's time for lunch, if you haven't already eaten in one of the museum restaurants or the outdoor cafés that dot the streets, hop on the trolley and go to Bull and Finch Pub (*Cheers*) at 84 Beacon Street, or the ever-popular Hard Rock

Café at 131 Clarendon Street. Both are grandchildren pleasers and I don't think you'll be disappointed either.

Consider These Day Trips

Salem is a must for your teenage grandchildren. They will revel in the witch hysteria described in the audiovisual presentation at the Salem Witch Museum. For those who have studied Nathaniel Hawthorne, don't leave Salem until you have seen his *House of the Seven Gables* with its secret passage. It was the author's home and is immortalized in his novel of the same name. Now a museum, it lends itself to an unforgettable visit.

If either of you would like to see where the American Revolution began, a trip to Lexington and Concord would be in order. The Lexington Visitor's Center across the Village Green contains a diorama of that first battle. You also may see the old bell that pealed the midnight alarm. On to Concord to see the North Bridge and there you can see where authors Louisa May Alcott, Ralph Waldo Emerson and Henry David Thoreau lived and wrote.

If your grandchildren are nearing college age, you certainly will want to take them around some of the famous schools in the area such as Harvard University, Radcliffe, Boston College and the Massachusetts Institute of Technology.

Before you leave Boston, be sure to take the express elevator to the 60th floor of the John Hancock Observatory for a panoramic view of the city that gave birth to the nation. See the sound and light show *The Road to Independence* and be transported back in time to Colonial days. Return to the present by looking down on busy Boston Harbor, the mingling maze of one-way streets and the mix of skyscrapers and brownstones. "Wonder how much it will be changed when I bring my grandchildren back here?" John mused half to himself as he looked out over the city. I wonder, too.

MAINE

The coast of Maine is dotted with beautiful beaches and beautiful resorts. All have their own individual charm. You probably can't go wrong with any one of them.

> ❝ Wonder how much it will be changed when I bring my grandchildren back here?" John mused half to himself as he looked out over the city. I wonder, too. ❞

Old Orchard Beach is a favorite of ours and I'm not sure why. Maybe because the beach is a seven-mile white sand strip and, since the surf is low, swimming is good. Maybe it is the fog that often rolls in so thick you can't see the ocean from the beach and the whole scene becomes eerie and mysterious. Maybe because life is so unhurried here and activities like biking along the streets are safe and fun. Maybe because the restaurants are charming and the food, especially the lobster, is excellent and moderately priced.

Whatever our reasons, I suggest you try it and see how much you like it. If you don't, move just a few miles north or south and try another. I guarantee you won't leave Maine until you have found the beach of your dreams.

NEW HAMPSHIRE

A three-hour scenic railway trip takes passengers from Bretton Woods to the top of Mount Washington, renowned as the highest peak in the Northeast, daily 8 to 8 from the middle of July through Labor Day. Times vary the rest of the year and, since advance tickets are recommended, it would be wise to call before you go. Phone (800) 922-8825 or (603) 278-5404.

There also is a road leading to the summit, but I don't recommend it because of the steep grades and sharp curves. If you decide to drive, be sure to listen and abide by the driving instructions given at the toll house. The mountain is also accessible by foot, butI'm not about to attempt that, with or without grandchildren.

Weather on Mount Washington is unusual. It literally can change in minutes from balmy to subfreezing. The wind velocity can be fierce, but views on a clear day are spectacular. You can see most of New England, some of eastern Canada and the Atlantic Ocean. Regardless of when you go, you're due for an adventure.

VERMONT
One New England resort and residential town of great charm is Woodstock. This town is noted for its well-preserved old houses, sugaring and village green. If you visit on a Sunday, pay special attention to the church bells that were cast in Boston either by Paul Revere or a family member.

East of Woodstock over the Taftsville covered bridge is Sugarbush Farm, a working farm that produces cheese and maple syrup. Visitors are welcome to view their processing daily 9:30 to 5 May through December. There is no admission charge.

In town, just across the Elm Street bridge, is the Billings Farm and Museum. Here, you can see what Vermont farm life near the turn of the 19th century was like before observing the workings of a modern-day dairy farm. It is open daily 10 to 5 May through October. There is an admission fee. Overnight accommodations include several restored historic bed and breakfasts.

CONNECTICUT
So your grandchild is fascinated with submarines? Don't hesitate to visit Groton, where the USS *Nautilus*, the first atomic-powered submarine, was built and is permanently displayed.

At the *Nautilus* on the naval base, you may take an interesting self-guided tour of this famous submarine. It is open Wednesday through Monday 9 to 5, but is closed New Year's Day and the first two weeks of May and October for maintenance. You may want to call ahead to be sure it is open when you plan to be there: (800) 343-0079. Admission is free.

At the Submarine Force Library and Museum, located at the other end of the pier, you will find films showing submarine development from the Revolutionary War to the present. The opening dates are approximately those of the museum. Again, you may want to call ahead at (800) 343-0079.

While in Groton, check with Project Oceanology located at the Avery Point Campus of the University of Connecticut about its cruises aboard its research vessel, the *Envirolab*. Three-hour cruises leave from nearby Fisher's Island Sound daily from late June through Labor Day. Reservations are necessary. Call (800) 364-8472 outside of Connecticut. Passengers learn how to measure lobsters, test seawater, identify fish and take samples from the ocean floor.

RHODE ISLAND

Many people, including teenagers, are very interested in learning about the rich and famous. There's no better way to do this than to visit the magnificent estates in the resort city of Newport. Go to the Newport County Convention and Visitors Bureau, 23 America's Cup Ave., for maps and information on the walking tours, audiotape tours, schedules and admission charges of the mansions. Many of the homes offer both individual and combination tickets. Buses for Viking Tours of Newport leave from the Convention Center also. Your teenager may never be happy back at home after she has visited these luxurious homes. But try it anyway - it promises a fun time.

CHAPTER 5

CALIFORNIA
AND THE WEST

Visiting California with your grandchildren, either boys or girls, is best when they are 8 or older. In the minds of many children, California is a fantasyland - a vivid kaleidoscope of blue skies, sun, sand, sea, snow and mountains, as well as a bright dream filled with desert, redwoods, flowers, mansions, swimming pools, beautiful people, movie stars, TV stars, fast cars and earthquakes. And it's a state that every child I know - 6 years and up - longs to visit.

I don't for one moment suggest you try to show your grandchild the entire state. It is far too large and diverse. Select one area, possibly two, that includes much that you both want to share and zero in on that.

SAN DIEGO

A favorite city of mine, not only because of its wonderful weather and distinct Mexican flavor, San Diego is also easy to get around in. It is a driver-friendly city with well-marked streets and interstates. Most points of interest are within easy freeway access. I think the best way to see this city is by car.

If, however, you choose not to drive, a good way to see the interesting sights is to take one or more of the bus or trolley tours. Gray Line Tours offers more than 15 trips and has pickup service from most major hotels. San Diego Mini-Tours has a variety of arranged bus tours including trips to Tijuana,

Mexico. Old Town Trolley Tours has two-hour excursions that visit Balboa Park, Gaslamp Quarter, Seaport Village, Old Town and Coronado, to name a few. You may board and reboard the trolleys at each stop. This is a good way to visit many of the places for as long as you choose and then reboard and continue with your sightseeing.

Since San Diego is built around a harbor, a boat tour is certainly in order. My 8-year-old granddaughter Phyllis was very taken with our cruise on the 38-foot sailing yacht *Soul Diversion* where all passengers (limited to six) are allowed to take the wheel and participate in the sailing. Reservations are required. Call (619) 224-0800.

When I take a grandchild to a city on the ocean, I always find it to our advantage and pleasure to find beachside accommodations. It's great fun to run in and out of the water, look for shells and participate in beach activities that appeal to both of you.

World famous for its size and rare specimens,

the San Diego Zoo is tops on the visiting list

for children and adults alike.

In the center of the city is an oasis of culture - beautiful Balboa Park. Here, 1,200 acres of art galleries, restaurants, museums, theaters and garden walkways make for a fascinating day. It was the site of the Panama-California International Exposition in 1915 and many of the Spanish Renaissance exhibit halls still remain. The park's most prominent feature is the 200-foot California Tower, which contains a 100-bell carillon that chimes every 15 minutes.

World famous for its size and rare specimens, the San Diego Zoo is tops on the visiting list for children and adults alike. It houses more than 4,000 animals, many in enclosures closely resembling their natural habitats. The Ituri Forest viewed through a huge picture window looks very much like an African marsh. Moving sidewalks take you into deep canyons and the Skyfari aerial tramway runs from the entrance to the Horn and Hoof Mesa, giving viewers a panoramic view of the zoo.

There's a double-decker bus that takes visitors through the maze of winding roads. I strongly suggest that you purchase the deluxe ticket; it includes admissions, bus and aerial tours and entrance to the Children's Zoo. You won't want to miss this; children have the chance to pet the gentler animals and see the newborn nursery. Special live shows are presented daily at the Wegeforth Bowl and Hunte Amphitheater. The zoo opens at 9 in the morning, and I recommend that you plan to arrive early and stay late. It will be a delightful day.

Cabrillo National Monument on Point Loma overlooks the city and the harbor. This is an excellent vantage point for viewing the herds of Pacific gray whales as they migrate to the Baja waters from Alaska between December and February. In case you aren't in San Diego during the winter months, you can see Shamu in a killer-whale show at SeaWorld San Diego. Beluga whales, sea lions, dolphins and walruses also are included in other enjoyable shows.

The Children's Museum (Museo de Los Niños) is a grand, hands-on adventure. The Improv Theater has costumes and a stage for role-playing, while other creative youngsters are introduced to paint and clay.

Don't fail to take a ferry, bus or drive across to Coronado to have Sunday brunch at the historic, magnificent Hotel Del Coronado. It's worth a visit and a tour, even if it isn't on a Sunday.

No visit to San Diego would be complete without a bus tour across the international border to Tijuana, Mexico. Driving is not recommended because United States automobile insurance is not valid in Mexico. Be sure to take bottled water and any snacks you might want. Eating and drinking in Tijuana is not a good idea, but attending a jai alai game and souvenir shopping are terrific.

For the sports-minded youngster, be sure to check the season schedules for a San Diego Padres baseball game or a Chargers football game.

If your grandchild is disappointed that he didn't sample true Mexican tacos in Tijuana, you may want to visit Old Town and try them at the Old Town Mexican Café and Cantina. This restaurant is on San Diego Avenue and, while you're there, you may want to take a walking tour of Old Town with its old adobe structures and quaint shops. State park rangers offer walking tours daily through this historic area.

Bidding farewell to this birthplace of California will not be easy. The memory of its people and its laid-back charm will stay with you for a long time.

SAN FRANCISCO

Take your grandchildren, boys and girls 10 and older, with you to San Francisco, where you won't need a car. Take a city bus tour, locate the places where you want to spend time and *walk*. The city center is compact enough that you can see almost everything on foot. Certainly the hills are steep and plenty, but the cable cars run frequently if your legs just can't take another step. The fare is only $2.

Fisherman's Wharf or Union Square is where you want to stay. From either area, you can get anywhere you want to go. You can catch a Tower Deluxe City tour for an overview of the city, catch the Blue and Gold Fleet to Alcatraz Island and the "Rock" from Pier 41, stroll about Pier 39 to watch street performers and mimes, and browse through unique little shops. Be sure to walk out on Pier 39 to watch the sea lions sunning themselves on the K dock. These marine creatures lived on the rocks below Cliff House some distance away for many years until the earthquake of 1989. After that they left the Cliff rocks and came to Pier 39 where they've made themselves at home.

Also at Pier 39 is the Citibank Cinema that shows the movie *San Francisco: The Great Adventure*. Down at Pier 45 you can board the USS *Pampanito*, a World War II submarine. There are other old vessels that your grandchild may enjoy exploring at the Hyde Street Pier and Pier 43-2.

Your city bus tour likely will stop for a bit at Golden Gate Park. You'll love having tea in the charming teahouse of the Japanese Tea Garden. And as you ride between Hyde and Leavenworth streets, look up Lombard Street, known as "the crookedest street in the world."

When you go to Alcatraz Island, be sure to take the park ranger tour. The ranger will tell you stories and show you the special cells where such notorious criminals as Al Capone and the "Birdman of Alcatraz" were incarcerated. It will make your trip more meaningful.

Chinatown is a city within a city. More Chinese people live here than any other place outside China and Hong Kong. Walk down Grant Avenue and savor the wonderful culture. Stop in the shops. Have tea in a tearoom. You can do this on your own or join the Wok Wiz walking tour. The fee for the walking tour and lunch is $39 for adults; call (415) 981-8989 for more details.

Be sure to eat in the famous restaurants on Fisherman's Wharf where they say the food is as good as the view - and I agree. Encourage your grandchild to try the seafood with which he is not familiar. However, you may regret this, as I did when I insisted that my granddaughter try lobster - a first for her. She was less than eager, but did comply with my wishes. She loved it and wanted to order it at every meal while there, much to the detriment of my budget.

Be sure to take a bus across the famous Golden Gate Bridge. You may want to take a cruise under it, too. The views are spectacular, as are those on the crests of the many hills. When your time is up in San Francisco, you may easily understand why Rudyard Kipling wrote "San Francisco has only one drawback - 'tis hard to leave."

Encourage your grandchild to try the seafood with which he is not familiar. However, you may regret this, as I did when I insisted that my granddaughter try lobster - a first for her. She was less than eager, but did comply with my wishes. She loved it and wanted to order it at every meal while there, much to the detriment of my budget.

LOS ANGELES

Rather than randomly going from one area of the city to another, decide with your grandchild the things you want to see and do before you leave home to visit Los Angeles. Make your hotel reservations in the general area of most of your priority attractions and, when you get to the hotel, let them arrange a rental car for you. If you need to change locations during your stay, find another hotel and go through the same procedure.

My 12-year old granddaughter wanted to see Hollywood, CBS and Universal Studios Hollywood, La Brea Tar Pits, the movie stars' homes, Mann's Chinese Theatre and the beach at Malibu. After checking in to our hotel, we asked about car rental, and the rental agency delivered a car to us the next morning. That night we pored over the map, decided on our route, made a few referral notes and were off early the next day. We repeated this procedure for the duration of our stay.

We drove to Burbank where we had a tour of the NBC Studios. During the Warner Bros. Studios VIP Tour, we saw the TV studios and the recording stages. We went on to Beverly Hills and Hollywood, where we boarded a Starline Tours of Hollywood sightseeing bus that took us to the Tar Pits, Mann's Chinese Theater and a tour of the stars' homes.

We spent another entire day at Universal City and another two days on the beach at Malibu. During the remainder of the week, we returned to places we'd seen on the tour but wanted to spend more time on than the tour allotted. By the end of the week, we had seen all of her priorities. We did it with a maximum of planning and a minimum of effort.

Los Angeles is not the place to bring a very young grandchild. It is very helpful to have someone along who can read your notes for directions and help watch for exit signs. But it is a beautiful and exciting city and one to which you will want to return many times.

YELLOWSTONE AND GRAND TETON NATIONAL PARKS

In all the rugged grandeur of the Rockies, there is no place more fascinating - to any age - than Yellowstone National Park. And nowhere else is more fun than Grand Teton National Park. Separated by only 60 miles, these two very different parks can be visited in one vacation. A trip to this area is appropriate with children 10 and older.

You probably will fly into Jackson, Wyo. This airport actually is within the boundaries of Grand Teton National Park so when you land, you are there. While there are shuttle buses that run between the parks, and tours within the parks, I strongly suggest you rent a car if at all possible so that you can come and go at your own pace.

Be sure to take your Golden Age Passport for $10 admission to both parks. If you're younger than 62, arrange for your discounted National Park pass at any national park or AAA office. Also, don't forget hiking boots for you and your grandchild. Even those who say they are non-hikers will find comfortable boots a necessity for the amount of walking you'll do.

I recommend that you plan to circle Yellowstone National Park first, then come back and spend the remainder of your time at Grand Teton. Before you leave for this geological wonderland though, I need to warn you to keep a close watch on your grandchildren while in the park. There are safe, established boardwalks between and next to the bursts of scalding water and bubbling mud pools in some thermal areas. Just be certain you and those in your charge stay on these walkways at all times.

Another warning, which you will see posted

throughout the park but which can't be emphasized

*too much, is **Do Not Feed or Touch the Wildlife.***

Another warning, which you will see posted throughout the park but which can't be emphasized too much, is **Do Not Feed or Touch the Wildlife.** These animals are wild and should be viewed only from a distance. Don't allow any hopping out of the car to take a picture of that cute bear cub. Remember that the mother bear is nearby and you could find yourself in a potentially dangerous situation.

The drive from Jackson to Old Faithful Inn in Yellowstone takes about three hours, so you can judge whether to spend the night in Jackson or go on to Old Faithful that day. Spend at least one night in the gigantic, log-built Old Faithful Inn, possibly the most beautiful lodge in America. Reservations must be made far in advance for all the accommodations in both of these parks. Write to P.O. Box 165, Yellowstone Park, WY 82190-0165, call (307) 344-7311 or call your travel agent for assistance.

For more than a hundred years, Old Faithful geyser has been erupting every 78 minutes (with occasional exceptions). Because of its frequency, this is the most popular geyser in the park. Approximate schedules for its performance are displayed daily in the nearby visitor center. You will want to view this phenomenon several times during your visit.

Two miles of boardwalk lead from Old Faithful to scores of geysers in the area. The Grand Geyser bursts on the average of twice a day. For several minutes, this giant sends spurts of water some 200 feet into the air. Check the prediction of eruptions and see at least one. Near the end of the walkway is the deep-blue Morning Glory Pool, its color determined by the algae.

Leaving Old Faithful, take the loop road up past the Paint Pots, which are large, colorful springs of hot clay. Along the banks of the Firehole River, you will probably find bison grazing lazily. At the Midway Geyser Basin is the Grand Prismatic Spring. In the Norris Basin you need to take separate trails, one to see the Steamboat Geyser, the tallest in the world, and the other to see the Echimus Geyser. Take your time on this part of your journey. Make many stops and walk about the designated areas to really take in the wonder. Your grandchild will be fascinated. She may not be all that excited about the gorgeous mountain scenery, but she will be thrilled with the geological marvels.

It will take most of the day for you to arrive at Mammoth Hot Springs near the Montana line and the site of park headquarters. Well-marked trails let you be safe while you gaze at the crusty tier upon tier of colorful, steaming stone on the misty mountainside.

Back on the loop road heading east, you will come to Mount Washburn, the park's highest peak. If you're up to an all-day hike, the trek to the lookout tower is a most enjoyable one and the view of the ice-packed peaks of the Beartooth Mountains is spectacular. A shorter, more leisurely trail leads to the spray-drenched base of Tower Falls.

Turning south, the loop road leads alongside the Yellowstone River as it rushes and roars between the steep, mineral-stained cliffs and plummets over the narrow waterfall of the Grand Canyon of the Yellowstone. Vistas from both north and south are breathtaking, but the panorama from the north side of the canyon may have more appeal to your grandchild because of its proximity to stores and snack bars.

If you suddenly smell something reminiscent of a garbage dump, it is probably the Mud Volcano, certainly the ugliest and most foul smelling in the thermal region. For the brave at heart (or those with little or no olfactory sense), you may want to take the mile-long boardwalk over smelly mud to the bare shores of Sour Lake.

Only a short distance south, you will come upon the crystal-line beauty of Yellowstone Lake, North America's largest alpine lake. Cruises, rowboats, motor launches and fishing expeditions are for hire, so take your pick and enjoy.

Hiking is a favorite activity in these parts,

certainly because of the stunning views at every

turn in the trail. An easy and popular walk

is along the shore of Leigh Lake under

imposing 12,000-foot Mount Moran.

Leaving Yellowstone and driving the few miles through a dense, green forest, you again enter Grand Teton National Park. Now is the time for you and your grandchild to relax, really get acquainted and have fun with each other in one of the most beautiful spots in the world. Regardless of your interests, you will find things you both enjoy.

Hiking is a favorite activity in these parts, certainly because of the stunning views at every turn in the trail. An easy and popular walk is along the shore of Leigh Lake under imposing 12,000-foot Mount Moran. Another hike circles the south shore of Jenny Lake to Hidden Falls. If you're particularly adventurous, you might consider the five-mile trek from Lupine Meadows to the tree line. It is strenuous, believe me, but the view of the amphitheater and Surprise Lake is stunning.

The roads around Jackson Hole are flat, so bicycling becomes a wonderful activity. Even if you haven't ridden for years, you'll soon realize it is something you never forget and you'll have a great teacher in your grandchild. Bikes are for rent in Jackson.

A must is to take a raft trip down the Snake River. Whether you opt for the scenic, the exciting whitewater, the luncheon trip or the evening wildlife, it's up to you. I guarantee you'll have fun.

Riding horses especially bred for the mountain terrain is a wonderful way to explore the park. If you aren't comfortable on a horse, you may prefer a wagon-train ride with dinner along the trail.

There are many companies that sponsor these activities. Shop around or ask at your hotel about availability and price of those that interest you. This is a different and exciting trip. It is one that can be very bonding - grandchild to grandparent - and will live in memory long after the photographs have faded.

MONTANA

Before you leave Yellowstone, you may want to take a side trip to the scene of the Battle of Little Big Horn, especially if you have a youngster who revels in the history of the Old West.

From Mammoth Hot Springs, take US 89 out the northern entrance to Yellowstone through Gardiner to Livingston, once the home of Calamity Jane. Turn east at Livingston and take I-90 to Hardin. Then follow the signs to the main entrance to Little Bighorn Battlefield National Monument about 15 miles southeast.

If you've forgotten the dramatic story of Lt. Col. George A. Custer and his 210-man Seventh Cavalry Regiment and thousands of Northern Cheyenne, Lakota, Arapaho and Sioux in the Valley of the Little Bighorn River, don't despair. You'll be able to pick up an audiotape in the visitor center and take a self-guided tour in your car or take a bus tour with the park ranger as your guide.

Better yet, plan to be in Hardin on the weekend closest to June 25 to watch a reenactment of the battle during the annual Little Big Horn Days.

IDAHO
Another offshoot from Yellowstone leads you into Idaho. For any grandparents or grandchildren who dream of walking on the moon, exit the west entrance and follow highways 26 and 20 to Craters of the Moon National Monument. It is 18 miles west of Arco.

Massive volcanic eruptions thousands of years ago have left enormous lava fields dotted with cinder cones of all sizes, the largest being 700 feet high. Huge vents resembling lunar craters zigzag across the 83-square-mile area. You will want to drive the seven-mile loop with many stops along the way (during the summer only). Wear sturdy shoes. The terrain is rough. When you come to the cave area, be sure to take along your flashlight for exploring the lava tubes.

OREGON

A young photographer, artist or naturalist will find Crater Lake National Park, off I-5 and on SR 62 in southern Oregon, a true paradise. The lake was formed by a volcanic eruption 7,000 years ago. The eruption caused the mountaintop to collapse, thereby creating a caldera, which in time filled with water. The result is the nation's deepest and, as far as I'm concerned, the most beautiful, brilliant blue lake I've ever seen.

From the southern entrance (don't forget to have your Golden Age Pass to avoid the $10 private-vehicle fee), go to the Rim Village Visitor Center. This is the starting point for several hiking trails within the park. One that may be of interest to you and your naturalist grandchild is the Castle Crest Wildflower Trail. It is known for its abundance and variety of wildflowers.

A 33-mile Rim Drive completely encircles the caldera that contains the lake. Parking is provided for towed trailers, which are not recommended on this drive. There are many lookouts along the way for marvelous photographic opportunities. The one I like best is Cloudcap on the east rim. Watch for the signs and drive about three-quarters of a mile off the drive. My grandson chose another site at Kerr Notch about eight miles east on Rim Drive. From here you can see the "Phantom Ship," which is a lava dike rising from the lake that resembles a sailing ship.

I cannot recommend taking one of the hourly boat tours. While I'm certain the scenery would be spectacular, Cleetwood Trail, only one mile in length from the parking lot to the dock, is extremely steep and far too dangerous for me and my grandson - much to the disappointment of my grandson.

NEVADA

In eastern Nevada not far from the Utah line is a series of old mining camps and ghost towns ripe for exploring. You may tour on your own, branching out from Ely, the center for mining and recreation in the area, but I suggest you go on a summer weekend and take the Ghost Train of Old Ely. Leaving from Ely's Nevada Northern Railway Museum, the train takes a two-hour tour through ghost town Lane City, Robinson Canyon and the Keystone mining district. If you want to go back and explore these places at a more leisurely pace on your own, you can do so at a later time. But I think you'll find this old train charming. It consists of several Nevada Northern Railway cars, including a flatcar, baggage car and Pullman coach pulled by a turn-of-the-19th-century steam engine. You may want to wear protective eye and head gear, especially if you ride in the flatcar, because of the coal cinders spewed in the air.

Other interesting ghost towns in the area are Hamilton, Cherry Creek, Taylor and Ward, and you can obtain information about them at the Nevada Northern Railway Museum.

UTAH AND COLORADO

If your grandchildren love the movie *Jurassic Park,* and if they know the names of the many dinosaurs, and if they can tell you whether a brontosaurus was a herbivore, a carnivore or an omnivore, then you need to take them to Dinosaur National Monument.

Straddling the state line near the northeast corner of Utah and the northwest corner of Colorado, this 325-square-mile area contains one of the world's largest concentrations of fossilized dinosaur bones. While many of the exhumed skeletons - some were complete - have been removed and are exhibited in museums of history across the nation, others have been left in place for visitors to see.

Seven miles north of Jensen, Utah, is the Dinosaur Quarry Visitor Center that encloses many of the dinosaur bones. There are exhibits illustrating the history of the quarry and the dinosaurs buried in it. A shuttle bus can take you from the center to the quarry daily 8:30 to 6 during the summer.

If you like, you can take a one-day or a five-day boat trip through the monument from the middle of May through September. Check with the rangers at the Quarry Visitor Center.

The Colorado Visitor Center on Highway 40, two miles east of Dinosaur, Colo., has more exhibits, lectures and an excellent audiovisual program. From this center, you can drive north for about 30 miles into the heart of canyon country. There are no fossil bones here, but it is in the canyon country where these great animals once lived. The scenery is spectacular. There are hiking trails and campgrounds.

WASHINGTON

It is quite doubtful that your grandchildren will know about Mount St. Helens, which awoke from a 123-year nap and erupted in 1980. That isn't likely to diminish their interest in an active volcano, however. Their interest will be piqued when they learn that, although dormant since the great blow, subtle seismic episodes indicate that the volcano might not be ready for another snooze.

While you're on Interstate 5, stop at Castle Rock and experience the eruption that blew the top and much of the bulging north face off this snow-capped mountain on the giant screen at Mount St. Helens Cinedome Theater. This will set the scene for your visit to Mount St. Helens National Volcanic Monument.

The visitor center, five miles east of I-5 at exit 49 on SR 504, is on the shore of Silver Lake. There is a very short trail outside the center that leads to a good view of Mount St. Helens, which is 34 miles to the east. Visitors are not allowed in areas close to the mountain. If you want information on hiking trails around the area, check with the information desk at the center.

SR 504 (Spirit Lake Memorial Highway) provides excellent views of the crater, the northwest lava dome and the blast zone. At Coldwater Ridge Visitor Center, you can watch a film relating to the eruption and the return of life to the devastated area. Mount St. Helens is only seven miles away from here. An even closer view (from five miles away) can be seen at Johnston Ridge Observatory, a few miles from Coldwater Ridge. Keep in mind that many of the roads are closed in winter.

If you're interested in a guided tour of the blast zone, you can contact Mount St. Helens Adventure Tours at (360) 274-6542. Thirty-minute to 90-minute helicopter flights also are available from several area airports. Check with the information centers.

NORTH DAKOTA

The 70,500-acre Theodore Roosevelt National Park in the Bad-lands of North Dakota is divided into sections. The south part is near Medora off Interstate 94, the north is near Watford City and the Elkhorn Ranch Site, which was established by Roose-velt, is midway between the two. A 36-mile loop drive begins and ends at the entrance of the south unit and a 14-mile drive begins at the north-unit entrance and ends at Oxbow Overlook.

Especially interesting to your grandchildren will be the herds of American bison that roam freely in both the north and south units. They can imagine Indians and early settlers hunting these huge creatures for their hides and meat.

Especially interesting to your grandchildren will be the herds of American bison that roam freely in both the north and south units. They can imagine Indians and early settlers hunting these huge creatures for their hides and meat. Bison hunting was the reason Theodore Roosevelt became interested in this area and sought to preserve it.

Young artists will enjoy the early mornings when the light changes the colors on the weird rock formations dotting the landscape. Young geologists will study the erosion made by the Little Missouri River and look for the burned-out coal and petrified wood throughout the area.

The Medora Visitor Center houses Roosevelt's first cabin, a museum and an orientation film. It is open daily 8 to 8 in the summer.

CHAPTER 6

WASHINGTON, D.C., AND THE MID-ATLANTIC

As the capital of our nation, Washington, D.C., should be one of the most beautiful and interesting cities in the world. And it is. No matter when you visit, you will find a wealth of special activities. The city is appropriate to visit with your grandchildren ages 7 and older. Many of the activities you'll find are geared especially for youngsters. The sights and events include:

✔ The Smithsonian Institution sponsors a kite festival on the grounds of the Washington Monument in late March or early April.

✔ An Easter egg roll takes place on the White House grounds, usually on the Monday after Easter Sunday.

✔ The biggest gala of all is the celebration of Independence Day, when there are parades, concerts and special events on the Mall. The festivities are capped off by a huge fireworks display at the Reflecting Pool near the Washington Monument.

Summers in Washington are hot and humid. Spring and fall have warm days and cool nights and it can be cold and blustery in winter.

With the exception of rush hours, driving an automobile in Washington is not that bad. The city is well planned and the streets for the most part well marked. Parking, however, is a big problem. For that reason, I suggest that, if you drive into the city, you should park the car at your hotel and leave it there. If you come by plane, forget about renting a car. Take the limousine to the hotel.

Public transportation is varied and excellent; sightseeing tours abound. There are bus, limousine, carriage, trolley and train tours.

Public transportation is varied and excellent; sightseeing tours abound. There are bus, limousine, carriage, trolley and train tours. The Metrorail is a clean, efficient subway system that seems to interest youngsters of any age. It provides access to most of the attractions and is very economical. Maps in each station give route and fare information. Avoid using taxis if at all possible.

Regardless of how you plan to get around, get a good city map and carry it with you at all times. Seeing this fine city requires walking. You can very easily become confused and go in the wrong direction without a map. Make sure, too, that you and your grandchild wear comfortable, well-broken-in shoes.

If you can, before you leave home, contact your state's senators and congressional representatives and get access to special tours of places like the White House, the Capitol and the House and Senate buildings. This may eliminate time-consuming and boring standing in line. You may be able to visit while Congress is in session. Most children and their elders enjoy seeing our elected representatives at work. Be sure to ask for passes to the House and Senate galleries when you write.

You need to make hotel reservations well in advance of your arrival. Your travel agent can assist you. Or, if you prefer, study the tour books and do it yourself. Nobody knows your interests and budget better than you do. AAA has excellent TourBook® guides, which are free to members. There is a wealth of other travel books available at AAA and in the bookstores. Browse through them and find one that fits your needs.

My suggestion is to select a hotel in the downtown area. It will eliminate precious travel time when you're sightseeing. Many tour buses routinely stop at the larger hotels. Virtually all of these hotels have family rates or discounts of one kind or another.

As far as I'm concerned, there is no better way to see Washington than to take the Old Town Trolley. It is a replica of a Victorian-era streetcar with a 90-minute narrated tour of the major attractions. You can board at many of the major downtown hotels. Tickets valid for one day cost $24 for adults and $8 for children 5-12. There are 18 designated stops including the Mall, Smithsonian Institution, White House, Embassy Row, Georgetown and Arlington National Cemetery. A trolley passes each stop every 30 minutes and you can get on and off as often as you wish.

On your first touring day, I suggest that you inquire at the hotel desk about when the first trolley pickup is. Then board and ride around the complete circle listening to the narration and deciding what you want to see first, then second and so on. According to the age and interests of your grandchild, you may want to eliminate certain places and devote your time to others.

Some must-sees for all ages, in my opinion, are the U.S. Capitol, the White House, Lincoln and Jefferson Memorials, at least two of the 13 museums of The Smithsonian Institution, Arlington National Cemetery, Mount Vernon, the National Zoo and the Washington Monument.

Although you'll have a wonderful time, you certainly can't see everything in one, two or even three days. Plan on a week, if at all possible. Your visit needs to include fun things as well as sightseeing. For example, grab a hot dog and soda from one of the sidewalk vendors after a morning of viewing monuments and institutions, and go paddleboating around the Tidal Basin.

If you didn't notify your congressional representative of your trip and didn't receive special access passes, you may want to consider a Gray Line Tour of the interior of the public buildings. There are several tours available. The morning tour includes stops at the White House, the Jefferson Memorial, Ford's Theater and the National Museum of American History. Tickets for the public rooms are included. Keep in mind that the White House is closed to the public on Sundays, Mondays and other days when there are special state events. If this is a high priority to you or your grandchild, you may want to check before you go. The Gray Line phone number is (802) 289-1995.

Another tour begins with a walking tour of the U.S. Capitol building. Hope you remembered to get your visitors gallery passes from your senator or representative. If Congress is in session, do stop, watch and listen. It is most interesting. The galleries are open 9 to 4:30 or when they adjourn. This tour also goes to the Supreme Court building and the National Air and Space Museum. You can buy separate tickets for the two tours. If you have gallery passes, you may want to bypass the afternoon tour and visit the other buildings on your own.

On the day you go to Mount Vernon, you may want to take a boat trip down the Potomac River. The *Potomac Spirit* leaves Pier 4 at Sixth and Water streets at 9 and 2 Tuesdays through Sundays and on occasional Mondays most of the year. This five-hour narrated cruise allows a two-hour stopover at George Washington's estate. Food is available on board. Reservations are recommended. Check the prices because they change frequently. Phone (202) 554-8000.

When you leave the trolley at Arlington National Cemetery, you may, of course, walk to any of the spots of interest in the cemetery. I suggest, however, that you purchase an inexpensive Tourmobile ticket. The Tourmobile shuttles you up to the Kennedy gravesites, the Tomb of the Unknown Soldiers and Arlington House. On the Tourmobile as on the trolley, you may get off the bus and reboard another at your leisure. Don't miss the hourly changing of the guard at the Tomb of the Unknown Soldiers and the eternal flame at President John F. Kennedy's grave.

I feel sure that, if you and your grandchild spent your entire vacation at the Smithsonian Institution, you would have a wonderful time and come away wishing you could have stayed longer. It's hard to believe that a man who was not an American and had never visited America founded this great institution. Yet it's true. James Smithson, a British scientist, willed his entire fortune to "found in Washington, under the name of the Smithsonian Institution, an establishment for the increase and diffusion of knowledge." Perhaps you should start or conclude your tour of the Smithsonian at the Castle that houses his tomb, just to say thanks.

I feel sure that, if you and your grandchild

spent your entire vacation at the Smithsonian Institution,

you would have a wonderful time and come away

wishing you could have stayed longer.

Also housed in the Castle are the administration of the museum, the information center, a turn-of-the-century children's room and two theaters that show orientation films. Most of the museums are open 10 to 5:30. For information about the day's events, call (202) 357-2700.

Meaningful Museums

The following museums seem to be favorites of most children and are located on the Mall in easy walking distance of each other. The National Air and Space Museum is at the top on my grandchildren's list. You can touch a moon rock and envision yourself in space. There are breathtaking IMAX films shown in a five-story movie theater. Charles Lindbergh's *Spirit of St. Louis* and the Wright brothers' Flyer are here. There is a planetarium where you can learn about anything imaginable concerning air and space. Free guided tours are offered daily at 10:15 and 1.

The National Museum of Natural History is for lovers of prehistoric culture and dinosaurs. A Children's Discovery Room is for hands-on learning. The fabulous Hope diamond is featured in an extraordinary collection. Guided tours are available.

The National Museum of American History began as the National Cabinet of Curiosities and has grown to contain items from nearly every facet of life. It was here on the second floor that my granddaughter Stephanie found the ruby-red slippers from *The Wizard of Oz*, which she talked about so incessantly that I was convinced for a while she'd seen nothing else.

In the Arts and Industries Building, you will find the Discovery Theater, which offers a variety of children's plays year-round. Call (202) 357-2700 for a schedule.

The best places in Washington for your youngster to shop for souvenirs are in the museum gift shops. Most have a wide array of interesting items at as reasonable a price as you can find. You might want to pass this on to your grandchild for whatever he thinks it is worth. Good, quick and inexpensive places for lunch are the various cafeterias and eateries in most museums and government buildings when you're sightseeing.

Part of the Smithsonian Institution, but located in Rock Creek Park, is the National Zoological Park. The grounds open at 6 a.m. and the buildings at 10 a.m. Closing time is 6 p.m. The indoor and outdoor exhibits house several thousands of animal species. Upon entering, check the hours for feeding times. Watching the animals being fed is always interesting, for child and adult alike.

The Bureau of Engraving and Printing, which prints money and stamps, is located just south of the Washington Monument grounds. It's interesting and free.

Near Union Station - one of the trolley's stops - is the Capitol Children's Museum. Here your youngster can touch and play with the exhibits, a learning experience that's fun. There are activities in the arts, theater, science, humanities and math. The children make crafts to take with them. There is a small admission charge.

Another hands-on program, this time pertaining to the exploration of the sea, storms and early life, is presented in Explorers Hall at the National Geographic Society. This free program is located in the Society at 17th and M streets NW.

Young artists or art lovers won't want to miss the National Gallery of Art at Fourth Street and Constitution Avenue NW or the Smithsonian American Art Museum in the Old Patent Office Building between Seventh and Ninth and F and G streets NW. The National Portrait Gallery is in the building's south wing. Check to ensure these galleries are open during the time of your visit.

For an excellent example of Gothic architecture, visit the Washington National Cathedral, which took 83 years to construct. One of the stained-glass windows contains a moon rock. Be sure to note the *Creation* window at the west entrance. It is pale blue in the morning, but by late afternoon as the sun moves across the sky and catches the red in the many glass prisms, its hue is completely changed.

Check a Washington newspaper for spectator sports or theater events while you're in town. There are often productions appropriate for children at Ford's Theater and the John F. Kennedy Center for the Performing Arts. If you go to Ford's Theater, detour across the street to the Petersen House, where Lincoln was taken after he was shot and where he died.

I purposely left mentioning the Washington Monument until now because I hope you will make this your very last stop before leaving the city. It is a memorable and fitting climax to visiting Washington, D.C.

I purposely left mentioning the Washington Monument until now because I hope you will make this your very last stop before leaving the city. It is a memorable and fitting climax to visiting Washington, D.C. If you leave on a Saturday or Sunday, you may want to drive there on your way out of town. You'll find adequate parking on these days. The monument is open daily 8 a.m. until midnight from April to Labor Day and 9 to 5 the rest of the year. The earlier you arrive in the morning, the shorter the line will be to enter. Expect a wait, though, but believe me, it is worth it, especially to see your youngster's reaction. My granddaughter was entranced when she looked out the first window of the observation room 500 feet above the city.

"Oh, look, Grandma," she called excitedly, "there's the White House and the Capitol." Running from one window to another she became more and more excited as she found the Castle of the Smithsonian, the Lincoln Memorial, the Mall, the

Reflecting Pool and on and on. We spent more than an hour going back and forth looking, remembering, saying goodbye. It was a wonderful end to a visit to our capital city.

VIRGINIA

Traveling through Virginia is virtually a nonstop history lesson. Your grandchild will never realize how much she is learning, she'll be having so much fun.

East of the state capital of Richmond lies the historic Tidewater Triangle, made up of Jamestown, Williamsburg and Yorktown, where the United States was born. Surrounding Richmond, which was once the capital of the Confederacy, are Civil War battlefields and memorials, as well as the homes of many famous Americans including George Washington, Thomas Jefferson, James Monroe and James Madison.

If you have elementary-age grandchildren, a driving trip through this beautiful state with stops in the mountains, at the beach and at historical spots he is interested in can be a wonderful experience.

NORTH CAROLINA

Strung along the North Carolina coast from near the Virginia line to Cape Lookout is a series of barrier islands called the Outer Banks. If you're looking for fine, warm-water beaches, you'll find them here.

Kitty Hawk is where the Wright brothers did their early flying experiments. Kill Devil Hills, where the Wright Brothers National Memorial stands, commemorates Orville's first powered flight in 1903. This is a great place to visit. So is Roanoke Island, the site of Sir Walter Raleigh's "Lost Colony." Nothing authentic survives on Roanoke, but three miles north of Manteo is an outdoor amphitheater where the impressive drama *The Lost Colony* is performed daily except Sunday at 8:30 p.m. This rates a good long "yes" and thumbs up by my grandchildren.

PENNSYLVANIA

Ten miles east of Pennsylvania's capital city of Harrisburg is Hershey. With streets named Cocoa and Chocolate and streetlights in the shape of Hershey's® kisses, it is indeed the chocolate capital of the America.

You can take an automated mini-train ride through Hershey's Chocolate World and see step by step how chocolate is made. At the end of the tour be sure to stop in the gift shop and gorge yourselves on an enormous chocolate sundae. Hersheypark®, which began in the early 1900s as a recreational park for the Hershey factory workers, is now a huge amusement park.

About an hour's drive up Highway 15 is Williamsport. Your grandchild undoubtedly will know about the town, even if you don't. Famous as host to the Little League World Series each August, it also has the Little League Baseball Museum, a must for any young baseball player.

DELAWARE AND MARYLAND

Rehoboth Beach, the nearest beach resort to Washington, D.C., is a favorite of ours, especially after days of sightseeing in the nation's capital. It appeals to my grandchildren, not only because of its wonderful, white beaches on the ocean and its accessibility to those of Rehoboth and Indian River bays, but also for the Funland amusements, which are so dear to youngsters' hearts.

Deep-sea fishing boats, which can be chartered, leave Lewes, just north of Rehoboth. Reservations are recommended but usually not necessary. Crabbing and clamming around the bays' beaches are fun for all ages. Surfing, too, can be enjoyed on the oceanside beaches. Other activities include a sandcastle building contest on the first Saturday in August and a Sea Witch Halloween Festival the last weekend of October.

If you love camping, the Delaware Seashore State Park on a seven-mile strip of land between the Atlantic Ocean and Rehoboth and Indian River bays is outstanding!

A grandchild approaching college age who might be interested in attending a service academy for college will appreciate a trip to Annapolis, state capital and home of the United States Naval Academy.

Guided walking tours of the Academy leave the Visitor Center inside gate one Monday through Saturday 10 to 3 and on Sunday noon to 3, March to May and the day after Labor Day until Thanksgiving weekend; and 11 to 1 December through February.

There is a museum in Preble Hall displaying a variety of relics including battle flags, weapons and ship models. Another section is dedicated to the naval astronauts.

Check with your guide as to when the next formal parade might be or even a noontime muster. These are very interesting to watch if you happen there at the right time. Every July 4 features a U.S. Naval Academy Band performance.

Annapolis is an old city, the first peacetime capital of the United States, and quite an interesting one. At the Historic Annapolis Foundation Museum at 77 Main Street, you can rent a tape player and audiocassette tape with Walter Cronkite taking you on a "Historic Annapolis Walk" (a tour to 19 historic sites).

WEST VIRGINIA

West Virginia is famous for its coal mines and furnishes much of the coal we use today. Just over the Virginia/West Virginia border is Bluefield, the southern anchor of the National Coal Heritage Trail. Here you'll find the Eastern Regional Coal Archives, which houses a collection of artifacts, diaries, photographs and mining equipment. If you and your grandkids are interested, pick up a guidebook and drive the Heritage Trail.

You can wend your way north on US 52 to SR 16 going north and east, passing company stores, miners' houses and railroad yards in 500 tiny company towns until the trail ends at Beckley. Mile markers along the way keep you abreast of the points of interest.

When you get to Beckley, you will be able to see workings of a mine at the Beckley Exhibition Coal Mine in New River City Park. Tours are available every half-hour daily 10 to 5:30 from April to November. Also in the park is a restored coal company house depicting the life of a coal miner and his family, and the Youth Museum of Southern West Virginia Theatre Mountain Homestead in four converted boxcars.

If you stay overnight in Beckley, don't miss Theater West Virginia, which offers a musical drama about those famous feuding families, the Hatfields and McCoys, in the Cliffside Amphitheater. The shows are presented at 8:30 p.m. Tuesday through Sunday from the second week of June until late August.

NEW JERSEY

Would your grandchild like to walk the beach Captain Kidd walked on so long ago? Does he long to climb the spiral staircase of a lighthouse and look out over the great Atlantic Ocean? Has he always wanted to see dolphin or whales in the sea? If your answer to any of these questions is yes, you may want to vacation at Cape May on the southeasternmost tip of New Jersey.

On one of our trips together, 6-year-old Katie and I were having breakfast on the restaurant patio overlooking the Atlantic Ocean when she suddenly became very excited, jumped from her seat and ran to the steps leading down to the beach. "Come on, Granny," she called.

Looking in the direction she was heading, I saw a school of dolphins cavorting in the clear waters just offshore. "Hurry,

Granny," Katie called as she ran toward the water. "Maybe we can catch one and take it home."

I saw a school of dolphins cavorting in the clear waters just offshore. "Hurry, Granny," Katie called as she ran toward the water. "Maybe we can catch one and take it home."

In April, there's a tulip festival, in May and June a music festival, and from June through September a summer theater. There is an observatory near Cape May Point State Park where migratory birds can be seen. Cape May Sunset and Dolphin Cruise and the *Schooner Yankee* offer cruises to sight whales and dolphins. Carriage and guided walking tours of the historic sites start at the Washington Street Mall.

See everything there is to see, play in the ocean, look for Captain Kidd's treasure - which I'm sure he buried along here - with your grandchild, relax and let the hypnotic ocean breezes lull you to sleep.

CHAPTER 7

FLORIDA AND
THE SOUTHEAST

With grandchildren in tow, my favorite part of Florida is the area from St. Augustine to Cocoa Beach. I have found this especially true when traveling with younger children. Sun, sand, surf, space and history abound along this stretch of the Sunshine State. Florida is great to visit with boys and girls 6 and older.

If you're flying to the state, the Jacksonville International Airport serves the northeast region. If you're coming by car, you will probably enter on either Interstate 95, which runs north and south, or I-10, which comes from the west. Amtrak also schedules stops in Jacksonville.

Train rides can be true adventures for kids of all ages. Regardless of how you arrive, you will need a car for the rest of your trip. Get directions to Jacksonville Beach, pick up A1A at the beach and drive down the coast for about an hour to the oldest European city in the United States.

ST. AUGUSTINE
What child isn't fascinated with the "oldest" this and the "first" that? This city contains it all - the oldest house, the oldest store, the oldest wooden schoolhouse. There's also a fountain that legend tells us is the Fountain of Youth. One drink of the spring water and you'll never grow old. Overlooking the

water is a massive old Spanish fortress with a moat, cannons and 33-foot walls for children to explore on their own.

What child isn't fascinated with the "oldest" this and the "first" that? This city contains it all - the oldest house, the oldest store, the oldest wooden schoolhouse.

In addition to all this, just south of the city walls on Anastasia Island are miles of wide, beautiful sand beaches on the Atlantic Ocean.

When you arrive in St. Augustine, you may want to head straight to the Visitor Information Center on Castillo Drive and pick up a supply of brochures, maps and information about the area before checking into your hotel. This way you can leisurely plan how and what to see during your visit.

One decision you will need to make before your trip is where to stay. Do you want to be on the beach? Do you prefer the historical area within walking distance of many sites, or inland where recreation is the strong point?

One day I was swimming in the motel pool with 5-year-old grandson John when a chubby youngster of comparable age came into the pool. The two boys struck up a conversation. "I can't swim without my water wings," the boy said. "My Uncle Joe says it's cause I'm too fat."

"Oh," John replied, "that shouldn't bother you. My Granny is fat and she's a good swimmer."

Parking in St. Augustine is at a premium. Please remember: A yellow painted curb means NO PARKING and the regulation is strictly enforced.

If you have a budding golfer, beginning tennis player or serious swimmer, you may opt to stay at one of the many resorts in this area that offer tennis courts, golf courses, pools and exercise equipment.

There is a walking tour starting at the Old City Gates and extending south on narrow St. George Street to the Oldest Store Museum, then back through the Plaza de la Constitucion. This is the best way to see the restoration of old St. Augustine. You may park your car at the visitor's center; none are allowed on St. George Street.

Allow at least three hours for a leisurely pace and photography stops and visits to points of interest along the way. Pause for a moment at the Spanish Bakery to sample the freshly baked meat turnovers, cookies and bread made from colonial recipes.

If you and your small charge prefer riding to walking, you can take one or more of six different open-air trolley tours offered by St. Augustine Historical Tours. Non-walkers also might choose the sightseeing trains that provide stop-offs at major points of interest. There also are colorful horse-drawn carriage rides that take you about the city in a fun manner.

One of the joys of childhood is exploring, and nothing is more fun for kids than running and poking about in a three-centuries-old fort. Park rangers at the Castillo de San Marcos National Monument provide an introductory talk and then you're on you own to peer into the garrison rooms and climb the stairway up to the gun deck, where cannons are fired Saturdays and Sundays from Memorial Day through Labor Day.

Regardless of your age, you won't want to miss drinking from Ponce de Leon's Fountain of Youth. On the same grounds are the remains of a Timacuan Indian burial ground.

At the historic Old Jail, costumed guides portray the early sheriff and his wife who take you through their living quarters and the prisoners' cells. Those who desire may sit in a replica of an electric chair.

For youngsters who have never seen an alligator and want to, try the St. Augustine Alligator Farm southeast on A1A.

There's a walkway to take you over and through a rookery and over an alligator swamp. Wildlife shows are presented hourly.

DAYTONA BEACH

Heading south once more on A1A, you'll soon come to Daytona Beach, famous for its 23-mile long, 500-foot-wide (at low tide) expanse of hard-packed white sand. Cars are allowed to drive along the packed sand at the water's edge in the daytime. In my opinion, this is not conducive to safe beach play for the children who love to run in and out of the water, fly kites and build sandcastles without having to be constantly on the watch for cars.

Despite this, I gave my grandchildren the experience of riding on the vast beach by paying the $5 toll and driving the car along the water's edge before saying farewell to Daytona Beach and continuing south toward the Space Coast.

Several miles south on US 1, you should turn east on Bennett Causeway. This will bring you to Merritt Island, Kennedy Space Center, Cape Canaveral Air Station, U.S. Space Camp Florida and Cocoa Beach. You should have made reservations for lodgings in Cocoa Beach, which has numerous good beachfront motels. But it's a very popular place, especially if you're fortunate enough to be there at Space Shuttle launch time. You may want to call NASA's shuttle hotline at (407) 867-4636 to ask for details about the next launch.

Six-year-old William and I were able to witness a lift-off from the balcony of our room. It certainly was an experience we won't forget. If you don't have a view of the launch site from your motel, a good spot for viewing is the Cocoa Beach Pier. The pier also has a very good restaurant, which is open daily for dinner and on Sunday for brunch as well. It's fun to eat looking out over the water.

To avoid crowds and ensure yourself admission to the theater and bus trip, you need to be at the Kennedy Space Center

Visitor Complex before the center's opening at 9 a.m. to buy your tickets. Allow a minimum of five hours to see the exhibits and theater presentation and to take the three-hour bus tour. If your grandchild is an astronaut wannabe as mine is, you may spend more than a day here.

Six-year-old William and I were able

to witness a lift-off from the balcony of our room.

It certainly was an experience

we won't forget.

Kennedy Space Center contains two IMAX theaters with different presentations and two bus tours. Nothing would satisfy my young aspiring astronaut but to return the second day and see everything, including the Air Force Space Museum, the Astronauts Memorial Space Mirror and, of course, the U.S. Space Camp, which he hopes to attend in a few years. This camp is great because it encourages the study of math and science in a fun, hands-on manner. We were able to watch the campers in the fourth to seventh grades undergo simulated space training, and we were allowed to experience *Mad Mission to Mars 2025*. I came away realizing that I had been born too soon.

FLORIDA'S SILVER SPRINGS

Rather than retrace your A1A route north to Jacksonville, I suggest you take Interstate 95 north to the exit at Highway 50 west, which intersects with the Florida Turnpike. Turn north on the Turnpike to Wildwood, where you will pick up I-75 north to Ocala, home of Florida's Silver Springs. This is about a three-hour drive.

There are several motels here, so finding good lodging even without advance notice shouldn't be a problem. I do suggest that you allot one full day to see Silver Springs®. If you have the afternoon of your arrival free, you might check out Blue Springs State Park. This is a great place to spot endangered manatees (depending on the time of year). Or, if you're brave enough, there is Wild Waters Park with a giant wave pool and eight water flume rides.

Silver Springs, estimated to be some 35,000 years old, was once a watering place for prehistoric animals. Fossilized remains of mastodons have been found in and around these artesian springs. This is of interest to most youngsters in this day when even kindergartners can identify dinosaurs by name.

There is an all-inclusive admission so plan to do it all - the glass-bottom boat, the Jungle Cruise, the Jeep Safari, the Lost River Voyage and the Doolittle Zoo. The hours are 10 to 5 daily with extended hours in the summer and on holidays.

Leaving Ocala and the Silver Springs area, you may choose your route back to Jacksonville. Highway 40 goes to Daytona Beach, where you can pick up I-95 north. Or if you want some more beach time, go over to A1A and retrace your earlier route. Highway 301 goes directly north, passing near Gainesville, home of the University of Florida, and traveling through Florida's range country. Turn east when you come to I-10 into Jacksonville where you can say a fond farewell to Florida . . . unless you want to visit more sights in the Sunshine State.

Maybe you are like I am and sometimes that inner child cries out to take the grandkids (several for this trip) to those wonderful places in the Orlando area where, regardless of your age, dreams come true. I've stated my beliefs that trips to amusement and theme parks should be taken by a mom and dad with the kids. And never would I want to replace an immediate family vacation, but there are so many wonderful things to do in Central Florida that likely couldn't be done in one visit, so . . .

ORLANDO

Let's say you've decided on the Walt Disney World® Resort family of theme parks. Don't head there without advance planning. Reservations at one of the Disney resort hotels should be made several months in advance. And, believe me, you do want to stay in the park. It may be a little more costly, but it will be worth its weight in gold and convenience. Free shuttles run constantly from the hotels to all the theme and water parks, Downtown Disney® and everything else on the expansive property.

Reservations at one of the Disney resort hotels should be made several months in advance. And, believe me, you do want to stay in the park.

Every day one of the parks opens an hour early for guests staying in the resort. You may buy Park Hopper® passes that have lower per-day costs than single-day tickets and allow entrance to the various parks day and night. You also qualify for FAST-PASSES℠, which give you a designated ride time for the most popular atractions.

As soon as you decide to go, I suggest you check with your travel agent, check your AAA Florida TourBook® guide, or go online to research the various Disney Resort hotels. If you're a budget-conscious grandparent as I am, you may want to look at Disney's All-Star Resorts. There are three different themes - sports, movies and music. Each boasts a large swimming pool, playground, coin laundry and food court, where even the pickiest grandchild is bound to find something he likes to eat. My favorite is Disney's All-Star Sports Resort, not because I'm such an avid sports fan, but because it's the first shuttle pickup and you'll always find room on board.

If at all possible, plan for a full week at the Walt Disney World® Resort. This way you won't exhaust yourself or your grandchildren. There's more than enough to do to keep everyone happy. You likely will want two days each in the Magic Kingdom® Park and Disney's Animal Kingdom® Theme Park. One day may be enough in Disney-MGM Studios and Epcot®, although I could visit at Epcot for the whole week. The seventh day should be spent at one of the water parks. My grandchildren love Disney's Blizzard Beach Water Park and we oftentimes end our day there in addition to the extra full day.

A word to the wise: Start your day early. The crowds are smaller, you and your youngsters are more energetic and it isn't as hot. Use your maps and plan your day before you start.

Remember, too, that all attractions may not be appropriate for your young charges even if they are tall enough or old enough, according to the signs. Some attractions are very fast and some are scary. You know your grandchildren. You be the judge.

I mistakenly took my 5-year-old grandson on the "Alien Encounter" attraction. He was terrified and it took several turns on the "It's a Small World" ride to calm him down. If you have a teenager who loves a thrill, check out the Twilight Zone "Tower of Terror" in Disney-MGM Studios. All ages will revel in stepping back into the dinosaur age at Disney's Animal Kingdom Theme Park. If it's a hot day and you're just back from the Kilimanjaro Safaris®, a ride on Kali River Rapids will cool you down in a hurry.

Last summer when William and his parents were swimming in the hotel pool at Walt Disney World, he was eager to show them how he had learned to float on his back while on his trip with Granny. "That's good," his mother said, "but if you keep your arms out straight, you might stay up longer." She said he paused, looked at her and said very positively. "My Granny taught me this way and this is the way I'm going to do it."

Universal Orlando and Islands of Adventure

Just off Interstate 4 at Turkey Lake Road are the two Universal Orlando^{sm} theme parks. You'll need to allow one full day for each park. Universal offers special packages with accommodations and guest privileges such as front-of-the-line access. Call (800) 711-0080 for additional information.

AAA members can buy a combination park ticket, which gives several consecutive days admission to Universal Studios, SeaWorld Orlando and Wet 'n Wild® Water Park; all are located in the International Drive tourist area. Busch Gardens® Tampa Bay, an hour-and-a-half away in Tampa, can be included in the admissions package.

Universal Studios gives an inside view of Hollywood with a working studio for TV and movie production. If your grandchildren are as addicted to the Nickelodeon® channel as mine are, you might inquire about possible participation in a live production that takes place here in the Nickelodeon Studios.

The rides are exciting and fun. Most children 8 and older will enjoy the startlingly realistic simulation of an earthquake and tornado. Next door in Islands of Adventure®, the favorite rides seem to be the Amazing Adventures of Spider Man and the Incredible Hulk Coaster. At the Jurassic Park River Adventure, dinosaurs pop out at you throughout the two-story ride.

SeaWorld Orlando

The spectacular marine-life adventure of SeaWorld Orlando is great for everyone in the family. Even if your youngsters have visited fine aquariums around the country, this is different. It includes close-up encounters with dolphins, stingrays and sea turtles; a dolphin nursery for newborns and their mothers; a large playground for children; and exhibits of penguins, manatees and other seldom-seen species.

A simulated helicopter ride takes you into a cool 68-degree Wild Arctic! exhibit where polar bears, walruses and beluga whales live side by side.

A variety of shows such as the Shamu Adventure featuring a killer whale and an eagle, a floorless roller coaster plunging its riders on a journey to the lost city of Atlantis and a performance of water skiing and other water activities make for an unusual and exciting day.

TAMPA AND BUSCH GARDENS
Driving southwest on Interstate 4, north on I-75, then west on Highway 582 brings you to Busch Gardens Tampa Bay, an African-theme animal park. The gigantic zoo features more than 2,500 animals in naturalistic settings. You can experience a Serengeti Safari Tour so realistic you'll believe you really are on the Dark Continent. There are exciting rides for all ages and a variety of shows all planned to please any generation. You'll need a full day to experience the fun at Busch Gardens Tampa Bay.

Clearwater Beach
Before you head north, you may want to spend some relaxing time on one of the beautiful Gulf of Mexico beaches, where the water usually is calmer than the ocean and the beaches are less cluttered.

If you haven't had a beach adventure with your grandchildren, it would be a great time to wind down, build sandcastles, hunt for shells and have picnics by the water. Clearwater Beach is easily accessible from Busch Gardens Tampa Bay and is a favorite of our family.

ALABAMA

Is one or more of your grandchildren a future space traveler or astronaut? Do you also harbor a secret desire to blast off? If so, take a trip to northeast Alabama and spend a day or more at the U.S. Space and Rocket Center in Huntsville. This is where space and rocketry began in the United States under the direction of Dr. Wernher von Braun.

The center houses one of the world's largest and most exciting exhibits of space and rocketry with hands-on activities to simulate space travel. There is an IMAX theater that shows hourly films, some of which were taken by the astronauts in space. Bus tours regularly leave here for NASA's Marshall Space Flight Center where you can see the astronaut training facilities, Spacelab stations and mission control.

You will need at least a full day to see and experience it all. The center's hours are 9 to 6. I suggest you plan on being there the whole time. While there you undoubtedly will see the campers at the U.S. Space Camp going through their paces as they simulate astronauts in training. Don't be surprised if your youngster cons you into sending him or her next year. It is truly a great experience for kids in grades four and up.

There are a couple of simulated space rides that I did not want William to see. I warned Katie and John, who had been there before, not to mention the ride because I feared William would be frightened. They promised they wouldn't and were true to their words, but just as we were leaving, William spied it and wanted to ride. I expressed my concern, but Katie assured me she could "take care of the boys," so, against my better judgment, I gave in to their pleas. Handing me their bags of souvenirs to hold, they stood patiently in the long line and finally entered the darkened space bubble as it began its jerking back and forth motion.

I knew my instinct had been correct when I saw William exiting the vehicle. Tears were slipping from under his tiny glasses and rolling down his cheeks as he ran to me. I picked him up and he whispered in my ear. "Next time let Katie hold the bags and you come with me." I promised I would.

On an Easter trip to Gulf Shores with her grandfather and me, 4-year-old Stephanie wanted to conduct an Easter egg hunt on the beach. Not taking into account the shifting sands, we hid the foil-wrapped candy eggs too well. She found very few. The following year when we returned, she immediately ran down to the water's edge and began to dig. "What are you looking for?" I asked. "The Easter eggs we left here last year," was her reply.

LOUISIANA

When you think of Louisiana, you probably think of New Orleans and French Quarter. Often called "Sin City," it is raucous, ribald, fun-loving and primarily an adult city. That doesn't mean you can't or shouldn't take your grandchildren. You can keep them safe and have a good time if you use common sense and act prudently.

First, I suggest you stay in the Garden District rather than the famous French Quarter. Of course, you'll want to take the kids through this historic area, but do it in the daytime and take a tour - don't walk.

The kids may not have been impressed with the Creole and Cajun food in New Orleans, but I guarantee they'll like those donut-like pastries - beignets.

The surreys, drawn by a mule in a flowered hat and driven by great storyteller drivers, are fascinating to all youngsters and a safe and excellent way to tour the French Quarter. Before you leave the French Quarter, you may want to visit the fine Aquarium of the Americas, which houses more than 15,000 creatures representing 530 species of marine life found throughout the Americas.

If you want to go to the zoo at Audubon Park, you will probably want to take the St. Charles Avenue Streetcar. Built in the 1920s, these olive-green streetcars are unique, making travel on them an adventure in itself. Because the streetcar cannot turn around at the end of the line, the passengers get off and the seats are reversed to face the other direction. The passengers then reboard and go back. The fare is quite reasonable.

Hamburger lovers will enjoy Camellia Grill at the turn of the trolley. You can sit at the bar and indulge in old-fashioned milkshakes, malts and "the best burger in the world."

MISSISSIPPI
Stretching for about 450 miles from Nashville, through some of Tennessee and Alabama and two-thirds of Mississippi is the Natchez Trace Parkway. A two-lane highway wends its way through the countryside at a leisurely pace, following as much as possible the Old Natchez Trace. It started as an Indian trail then evolved into a pioneer highway. This was the route Andrew Jackson took to New Orleans. It was a favorite of highwaymen who laid in wait for some prosperous-looking traveler to rob.

This route appeals to history buffs who would like to relive some of the events of the past in a slow and leisurely fashion without the usual tourist trappings. The speed limit is 50 mph. There are no towns.

Historical markers along the way tell the stories of the old Trace. There are trails that lead off to points of interest along the way. If you have a grandchild who revels in this type of thing, be sure to go.

You also will see the location of a Chickasaw Indian Village. You will visit the place where the explorer Meriwether Lewis died, either by his own hand or that of a murderer. One of the largest Indian mounds in the country lies just off the Trace near Natchez.

Take along a picnic basket - there are plenty of roadside picnic tables - and have yourself a peaceful, stress-free and inexpensive trip getting to know your grandchild.

Take along a picnic basket -

there are plenty of roadside picnic tables -

and have yourself a peaceful, stress-free and

inexpensive trip getting to know your grandchild.

Remember that you will have to exit the Trace for food, lodging and gas.

GEORGIA

Atlanta is a beautiful old Southern city destroyed by fire during the Civil War, only to rise to be the cosmopolitan center of the Southeast. I suggest three must-see places to visit with your grandchild. Grant Park, near the site of the Battle of Atlanta, contains the Cyclorama depicting this battle in a circular painting 42 feet high and 358 feet in circumference. Visitors sit on a revolving platform while listening to the narration as the sound and light effects enhance the three-dimensional figures. It is truly fascinating.

For lunch, dinner or a midafternoon hamburger, try the Varsity drive-in restaurant near Georgia Tech. It's a step back in time, for the Varsity has been in business more than a half century and remains unchanged in this city of change and growth.

Just east of Atlanta off I-285 rises a giant granite monolith 825 feet high and five miles in circumference. On the northern face, the figures of three Confederate heroes, President Jefferson Davis, Gen. Thomas "Stonewall Jackson" and Gen. Robert E. Lee, have been sculpted into the rock. There is a one-mile hiking trail up the west side to the summit and a five-mile historical trail leading around the mountain.

SOUTH CAROLINA

Have you told your grandchildren stories of the Civil War? Do they want to see where the war began? Then journey south to Charleston. Offshore of this lovely city is Fort Sumter, a manmade island on which a Union garrison stood in the early 1800s.

On April 12, 1861, Confederate troops opened fire on it and after two days of bombing, captured it, thereby signifying the onset of the Civil War. Now, national park rangers present history talks and conduct museum tours here at the Fort Sumter National Monument, which is accessible only by boat. Boat tours leave the Charleston City Marina three times a day April through Labor Day. Times vary during the remainder of the year. Be sure the boat tour you take stops at the fort; some only cruise the harbor.

CHAPTER 8

GREAT SMOKY MOUNTAINS NATIONAL PARK AND THE MIDWEST

A trip to the Great Smoky Mountains is perfect, but especially for your younger grandchildren. It has all sorts of fun and hands-on activities that are also learning experiences. Whether you live near enough to drive from home or choose to fly into the Knoxville Airport and rent a car, I truly believe you and your grandchild will thoroughly enjoy this memorable mountain experience.

One-third of the population of the entire United States live within a day's drive of the Great Smoky Mountains National Park, located on the border between Tennessee and North Carolina. This makes it one of the most popular tourist attractions and the most visited of all national parks. This visit is appropriate for you and your grandchildren age 5 and older.

This park is especially fun for younger children. I usually start taking mine when they are 4 or 5 years old. There are misty mountain trails to be explored, rocky rivers to be waded and ski lifts in Gatlinburg to carry you to the top of bluish mountain peaks. You can also enjoy the pioneer villages and a glitzy town with multitudinous hotels and motels, excellent restaurants, candy factories and souvenir shops.

Gatlinburg is where my grandchildren and I choose to stay. Nestled at the foot of Mount LeConte, stretching for about two miles on the banks of the Little Pigeon River, this glittery small town is fascinating to children. While the high degree of commercialization is a turn-off to some, my grandchildren and I love it. The narrow main street - Highway 441 - is thickly lined on both sides with hotels, motels, restaurants, shops, amusement parks and other attractions. It's a town where even younger children can feel a certain amount of freedom as they walk up and down the streets, dodging in and out of the shops and spending their vacation money.

This park is especially fun for younger children.

I usually start taking mine when they are

4 or 5 years old.

I suggest staying in one of the centrally located motels or hotels so that almost everything is within walking distance. You may also prefer an accommodation that has both indoor and outdoor swimming pools, so the kids can swim regardless of the weather. Gatlinburg is somewhat more expensive than its neighbors Sevierville and Pigeon Forge, but you can walk everywhere, the restaurants are far better and the atmosphere is more resort-like.

On the North Carolina side of the mountains just outside the park is an Indian reservation with an amphitheater showing a long-running drama. Nearby is a town where gems are found and panned for by tourists.

The first day in Gatlinburg is usually the best time to explore the town. Start by taking one or several of the 19th-century replica trolleys that carry passengers in and around Gatlinburg from April to Thanksgiving (winter scheules vary). Then, having selected and prioritized what you want to do and see, start walking. A word of warning: Be sure to set spending limits for yourself and your grandchild. It's very easy to go far over budget here in a short period of time.

Sometime that first day, you'll probably take the chairlift from the middle of town to the top of Crocket Mountain, have your picture taken, view the picturesque surroundings or opt for the observation tower at the corner of Airport Road. You undoubtedly will visit one of the candy factories to watch the way the sweet delights are made before sampling and perhaps buying some. The chocolate fudge is my favorite, but my grandchildren all favor the candied apples. Ambling in and out of the multitude of souvenir shops, stopping to play a game in an arcade or having your fortune told by a machine may take up most of your day.

The Aerial Tramway takes you the couple of miles from downtown to the Ober Gatlinburg complex where there's skiing in the winter, an ice skating rink, an alpine slide, a black bear habitat, a sightseeing chairlift to the 3,500-foot summit of Mount Harrison and cafés with live entertainment.

Be sure to check at the Gatlinburg Convention Center for any special events that might be going on while you're there. The Guinness World Records Museum is fascinating for the younger generation and you might pick up some trivia there, too.

Restaurants in Gatlinburg are abundant and, for the most part, good. Of course, you may be conned into eating at McDonald's®, Shoney's® or the Dairy Queen®, but if you can, negotiate with your grandchild and try some others, too.

I suggest you drive the few miles down to Sevierville one day to enjoy lunch in a flourishing apple orchard and go shopping at one of the several outlets you'll find as you drive back through Pigeon Forge toward Gatlinburg.

Take a full day for a trip down Little River Road to the 11-mile Cades Cove loop. Years ago, before the area was taken over by the National Park System, farm families carved homesteads in this wilderness. Preserved by the park, some of the old barns, rustic churches, mountain cabins and grist mills stand silent, allowing newer generations to take a peek at what life once was like in these mountains. Plan to spend time here, running about, exploring and imagining. On Wednesdays and Saturdays from dawn until 10 a.m., the loop is reserved for cyclists. You can rent bikes at the Cades Cove Campground.

On the way to or from Cades Cove, be sure to stop by Sugarlands Visitor Center to pick up leaflets and brochures covering the various nature trails, both for hiking and driving, the wildlife and any special activities.

On another **day**, head up US 441 into the park, go past Sugarlands and up the 13-mile drive to Newfound Gap on the North Carolina border. The scenery is spectacular, so stop to enjoy it. See the weird shapes of the chimney peaks towering above you. Watch along the road for black bears, remembering not to feed them or get out of the car when they're around. Pause to have a snack at a picnic area alongside the rocky river where you may want to doff your shoes and wade out in the cold, clear mountain stream. Take a short hike on one of the many trails leading to a special vista. You may run through some low-hanging clouds as you ascend the mountain. This is always fascinating to youngsters.

When you get to Newfound Gap, stop, get out of the car and gaze out over the bluish haze of these massive mountains. You'll understand how they got the name Smoky. You'll see the highway winding on down the North Carolina side - a road you will take one day soon when you visit the Qualla Boundary Cherokee Indian Reservation. See the entrance to the famed Appalachian Trail that wends its way from Georgia to Maine.

A seven-mile spur road leads from Newfound Gap to Clingmans Dome, the highest point in the park and in all of Tennessee. Take the half-mile trail up to the concrete spiral walkway tower from which you can survey the panorama spread below you.

When you're ready to bid farewell to Gatlinburg, retrace your route to Newfound Gap and continue down the mountain to

Cherokee, N.C., home of the descendants of the Cherokee Indians who in 1839 escaped into the mountains, thereby avoiding their forced removal over the infamous Trail of Tears to Oklahoma. *Unto These Hills* is the sad story of this tribe told dramatically in the outdoor mountainside theater nightly except Sunday. I strongly recommend it. Be prepared, though, for your grandchild to come away wanting to give back your land to the Indians. You'd be wise to check into one of the several motels along the highway rather than drive back over the mountain to Gatlinburg late at night.

Oconaluftee Indian Village is another must. It is a replica of a Native American village of more than 250 years ago. There's a storyteller in the seven-sided house, an herb garden and a variety of craft demonstrations all put on by authentic Cherokee Indians. My 4-year-old granddaughter was enthralled by the whole program. Having been told that the Indians in the souvenir shops on the highway were Indians but not true Cherokees, she staunchly refused to pose for a picture with one in a chieftain headdress outside a shop.

At the Museum of the Cherokee Indian, down the street from Oconoluftee, the Cherokees sell some of their traditional crafts, many of which you will have seen demonstrated in the village.

If you have a young rock collector with you, continue your trip south on US 441 to Franklin, N.C., the home of the Ruby Mines of Cowee Valley. There are several surface mines in the area. Most of them furnish information, equipment and assistance for those who want to search for gems. For about $5, you can purchase a pail of dirt to sift through a strainer to search for ruby, sapphire and other mineral chips and stones. There are gem shops in the area that will polish and mount the gems you find if you desire. You almost always find something and it's great fun. Every July and October, there's a Gemboree featuring jewelry and gem exhibits and ruby mining.

ARKANSAS

You don't have to be a rock hound to enjoy Craters of Diamonds State Park in Murfreesboro, but it helps to be a little greedy. Here you can search in an open field of diamond-bearing volcanic soil to your heart's content and keep any stones you find. This includes other semi-precious stones such as amethyst, quartz, agate and jasper. The park, which is the only productive deposit of diamonds in the United States, is open from 8 to 8 Memorial Day to Labor Day and 8 to 5 the rest of the year. Admission is $4.50.

You don't have to be a rock hound to enjoy

Craters of Diamonds State Park in Murfreesboro,

but it helps to be a little greedy.

You may bring your own garden tools for surface searching (they allow any tool which does not have wheels or a motor) or you can buy or rent tools there. Screens to sift the soil are for rent and there is water to filter the soil away from the minerals.

This is somewhere you may want to bring several grandchildren, even of various ages. It really is great fun for several of you to dig, scrape, wash and wonder if the next stone will be THE one.

On one trip to the Crater of Diamonds State Park, I took my two grandsons. We spent considerable time digging in the vast area of plowed earth in search of the precious stones and found innumerable samples of other interesting rocks. Each time one of the youngsters unearthed a stone, he would come running to me to ask if I thought it might be a diamond.

"Oh, I hope so," was my response, "but we'll have to wait until the park ranger can assess it to know for sure." When we finally finished our search and took our treasures to the ranger's office, I heard one of the boys quietly tell him. "Our Granny thinks all these are diamonds. She'll really be disappointed if they aren't."

Two diamonds were found the day my grandchildren and I were there. Regrettably, we were not the lucky ones. But we did find quartz, jasper, mica and lamproite, which were nice souvenirs for each of us. And most of all we had fun!

To get to the diamond crater, head southwest on Interstate 440 from Little Rock. Pick up I-30 for about 60 miles, then Highways 8 and 51 until you come to Highway 26 heading west. Continue about 30 miles to Murfreesboro.

SOUTH DAKOTA

It isn't served by Amtrak and has only two major airports. Yet, if you fly into Rapid City, you are only 24 miles northeast of Mount Rushmore National Memorial, where the world-famous faces of George Washington, Abraham Lincoln, Thomas Jefferson and Theodore Roosevelt are carved into the mountainside. And only 17 miles farther south is the unfinished massive granite carving of Crazy Horse.

Turn northwest from Rapid City and go for less than 50 miles to Deadwood, reputedly one of the wildest gold rush towns and burial place of Wild Bill Hickok and Calamity Jane. Farther north is Spearfish, famous for the Black Hills Passion Play, which is held three times a week throughout the summer.

Across the state, about 60 miles northwest of Sioux Falls, is the town of De Smet, known as the "Little Town on the Prairie." You may tour 18 of the sites Laura Ingalls Wilder mentions in her autobiographical books. Keep in mind, though, the TV location for the stories is in southeast Kansas near Independence.

KANSAS

Want to walk the "yellow brick road" and relive much of *The Wizard of Oz* with your grandchildren? Then plan a trip to Liberal during the third weekend of October when Octoberfest is patterned around the book.

Even if you can't make it at that time, you can visit Dorothy's House, a simulation of the one where Dorothy and Toto lived with Uncle Henry and Aunt Em. It's next door to the Coronado Museum. You will find the Liberal Convention and Tourism Bureau at One Yellow Brick Road.

MISSOURI

If you're driving to Missouri from the East, the first thing you'll see as you cross the great Mississippi River is the Gateway Arch towering over cosmopolitan St. Louis. The first thing you'll want to do is take the tram to the observation deck at the top of the arch and look over this "Gateway to the West" and its swiftly running river. It will take 30 to 40 minutes for the trip and you may have about an hour's wait, but it is worth it.

From there, according to your interests, you may want to go to the zoo; visit the St. Louis Children's Museum, which is also known as the "Magic House"; see the St. Louis Art Museum; or stop by poet Eugene Field's House and St. Louis Toy Museum. If you don't remember Eugene Field's nostalgic *Little Boy Blue* or *Wynken, Blynken and Nod*, it is likely your grandchild will. You may want to carry one of his books of poetry with you and read from it before or after you have seen his boyhood home.

If your grandchild is a baseball fan, arrange to be in St. Louis when the Cardinals are playing. It will be an unforgettable experience. Be sure to see the St. Louis Cardinals Hall of Fame Museum on the Walnut Street side of Busch Stadium while you are there. It stays open until 6:30 on game nights.

Lovers of Tom Sawyer, Huck Finn and Becky Thatcher may talk you into driving north along the Mississippi River to Hannibal to see where Samuel Clemens - Mark Twain - lived as a boy and which he later used as a setting for several of his books.

Lovers of Tom Sawyer, Huck Finn

and Becky Thatcher may talk you into driving north

along the Mississippi River to Hannibal to see where

Samuel Clemens - Mark Twain - lived as a boy

and which he later used as a setting for

several of his books.

KENTUCKY

Located near the center of the state of Kentucky off I-65 is Mammoth Cave National Park containing - as the name implies - a mammoth cave. If you have a young spelunker for a grandchild, he will love this long cavern, which contains more than 300 miles of underground passages on five levels. Some of the rooms are 200 feet wide. There is a dome 192 feet high and a pit 105 feet deep. Hollowed out by the seepage of groundwater and the flow of underground streams, Mammoth Cave contains a variety of different limestone formations.

Open year-round, Mammoth Cave features tours ranging from one to six hours. Prices and schedules are available at the visitor center. Wear sturdy shoes and carry a jacket or sweater. The temperature inside averages 54 degrees F, and the walkways can be wet and slippery. Be sure to see the informative movie shown in the visitor center before touring the cave. The tour will be much more meaningful if you do so.

ILLINOIS

Perhaps the first thing you will want to do when you arrive in Chicago is to go to the top of the 110-story Sears Tower, the tallest building in the United States. Here you can watch a short multimedia presentation about the Windy City and get an idea of where you are.

Next, I suggest that you and your grandchild take a bus tour of the city so you can set your priorities about what to see. You may opt for the Chicago Motor Coach Co. that offers sightseeing tours in English double-decker buses; this tour is always fun for the younger set, especially if you sit up top.

There are so many exciting things to do and see in this great city that you can't do it all in one visit, so decide what you want to see according to your time and your grandchild's interests. But please don't miss the Museum of Science and Industry. It is great for all ages. There are buttons to push, levers to lift, cranks to turn. There is a real German U-boat from World War II, a walk through the human heart, a replica of a working coal mine with an underground train and more than 3,000 other items.

Music, art and the theater are alive and well here. Lincoln Park Zoo is great - especially the Children's Zoo and Zoo Nursery. The oceanarium of John G. Shedd Aquarium is reputed to be the largest indoor marine pavilion in the world. And, of course, the string of beaches along Lake Michigan is there for your enjoyment.

INDIANA

Memorial Day is *the* day for your auto-racing-enthusiast grandchildren to visit Indianapolis, because it is here that the annual Indianapolis 500 race is held. Considered the biggest one-day sporting event in the world, it draws several hundred thousand fans to the Indianapolis Motor Speedway each year.

In case this is not your cup of tea, you might take your grand-child later in the summer. Granted, you won't see the race, but there is a Hall of Fame Museum inside the speedway oval. Here many of the winning cars and other racing memo-rabilia are on display. When weather permits and the track is not in use, bus tours around the track are available. There also is a film depicting the history and highlights of this race.

Other places of interest in Indianapolis are the Children's Museum and Cinedome Theater of Indianapolis, the Indian-apolis Zoo, and, for those who love James Whitcomb Riley's *Little Orphan Annie* and other marvelous poems - be sure to read them at home before you go - his home is open to the public Tuesday through Saturday from 10 until 4:30.

Before you leave Indianapolis, you may want to drop by the Hooks Historical Drug Store on the Indiana State Fairgrounds and indulge in an old-fashioned ice cream soda from the antique soda fountain still in operation.

OHIO

Just off Ohio's northern shore, between the cities of Toledo and Cleveland, lies South Bass Island in Lake Erie. It can be reached during the summer by automobile and passenger ferry from Catawba.

This area is famous for Perry's Victory and International Peace Memorial, commemorating the Battle of Lake Erie in the War of 1812. It was on Sept. 10, 1813, that Commodore Oliver Perry and his American fleet assembled on the British-held lake, met the British fleet and defeated it. A pivotal battle of the war, it made possible the recapture of Detroit and enabled Gen. William Henry Harrison's invasion of Canada. It was after this battle that Perry sent his famous message, "We have met the enemy and they are ours." Rising 350 feet, the memorial is made of pink granite and has an observation deck on top. At the Lake Erie Islands Historical Society Museum, you can learn far more of the Battle of Lake Erie through film and relics.

Don't leave the island before taking the train for a one-hour narrated tour of South Bass Island. Trains run every half-hour and you can get off any time and reboard at no additional cost.

NEBRASKA

Many years ago as the pioneers pushed their way across America, they came upon a huge 500-foot-high rock rising over the south bank of the North Platte River in western Nebraska. It marked the end of the prairies on their journey west. As time passed, this landmark continued to be an important spot, and Chimney Rock National Historic Site was established so future generations could see and appreciate the journey of our ancestors.

There is a two-mile paved road leaving SR 92. At the end of this, you must hike about a half-mile to the rock. It is especially beautiful at night when it is illuminated.

You need to stop in Bayard, which is almost in the shadow of Chimney Rock, and have an early-morning chuckwagon cookout with a covered wagon tour on the Oregon Trail. For those who really want the pioneer experience, there are covered wagon vacations lasting from one to six days. Reservations are required; call the Oregon Trail Wagon Train at (308) 586-1850.

IOWA

Almost due east of Des Moines is the little town of Pella, meaning "city of refuge." Settled in the mid-1800s by Dutch emigrants fleeing religious intolerance, it has been renovated to look like a town in the Netherlands. Here there's an animated musical town clock, the Klokkenspel, tulip gardens, Delft collections and a museum that contains a miniature Dutch village and offers wooden shoes for sale.

Tulip Time comes in May with the blooming of the tulips, of course; it is perhaps the largest festival in the area. The townspeople dress in Dutch attire for dancing, traditional street scrubbing and parades. Another Old World festival, Kernies, is held in July. The Fall Festival is held in September, and the Christmas Walk is staged Thanksgiving through the end of the year.

MINNESOTA

Most teenagers - and some preteens - I know love going to the mall, whether to shop or just hang out. Undoubtedly, a visit to the Mall of America in Bloomington, a suburb of Minneapolis, would make your teens think they had died and gone to heaven.

Undoubtedly, a visit to the Mall of America in Bloomington, a suburb of Minneapolis, would make your teens think they had died and gone to heaven.

Built on 78 acres, it has more than 500 specialty shops. The big stores include Macy's, Nordstrom's and Bloomingdale's, but there are a multitude of restaurants, a walk-through aquarium, a 14-theater movie house, a miniature golf course and the largest indoor family theme park in the United States. Shopping hours are 10 until 9:30 Monday through Saturday and 11 to 7 on Sundays.

MICHIGAN

Would you and your youngsters like to take a step back in time to visit an island where there are no motorized vehicles and where transportation is by horse-drawn carriage, bicycle or horse, and the only way to get there is by ferry, catamaran or plane?

Then Mackinac Island in the Straits of Mackinac between Michigan's Upper and Lower peninsulas is for you. The island, only three miles long and two miles wide, is a summer resort with a fabulous, historical Grand Hotel perched on a hill overlooking the joining of Lakes Michigan and Huron. Pricey it is, but don't worry, there are several other good hotels on the island. Or you may return to Mackinaw City if you choose. Be sure to take a carriage ride around the island and shop in the quaint little boutiques on the waterfront.

WISCONSIN

Near the center of the state - north of Madison, just off Interstate 90 - are the Wisconsin Dells, a unique and somewhat mystifying phenomenon. The Wisconsin River has cut out fantastic shapes in the soft sandstone cliffs for a distance of about 15 miles. It is indeed a young photographer's or geologist's dream.

A dam separates the river into the Upper and Lower Dells. The only way to really see and appreciate this marvel is to take one or both of the boat tours. On the Upper Dells tour, a two-hour tour through the sandstone cliffs, you'll see weird rock formations and have stops at Witches Gulch and Stand Rock, where you can hike the short nature trails. The one-hour nonstop Lower Dells tour takes you through more odd rock formations, caves and Rocky Islands.

Be aware that there are plenty of other tourist attractions here - mainly, I believe, to separate your grandchild from his money - and having little or nothing to do with this natural novelty.

TENNESSEE

If you are traveling with a grandchild age 4-10, don't overlook Chattanooga on the Tennessee-Georgia border. In the middle of downtown on the banks of the Tennessee River and at the foot of towering Lookout Mountain are many wonders for small children.

Take Market Street and follow the Tennessee Aquarium signs. There are several parking lots available in the area. The place my grandchildren always want to go to first is the Creative

Discovery Museum, just down the street from the aquarium. Here imagination reigns. Young archaeologists work in a simulated dig to uncover dinosaur relics. My little Shelby loves painting her own face as well as the clay figures she creates. The museum opens at 10 in the morning. I suggest you be there at that time. It is less crowded and easier for your youngster to move from one exhibit to another. Plan to spend a few hours here.

Then go back up the street to the four-story Tennessee Aquarium, a state-of-the-art home to more than 9,000 fish, reptiles, amphibians, birds and mammals. An escalator takes you up to the top of the building where you start your self-guided tour, winds down wide ramps past the many simulated environments. Here, too, you have the freedom to move as slowly or as quickly as you choose. Check with the assistants there as to feeding time for the sharks and other animals.

Across the street from the aquarium is the massive theater that shows a breathtaking IMAX movie. Some of these films are wonderful for young children, but others may be a little too mature for them. I have seen one on dinosaurs and another on dolphins, which my grandchildren loved, but there was one on space that I wish we had skipped. It was more appropriate for the teenagers.

There are several nice restaurants in the area, but if you really want to please your grandkids and top off a fun day, try the Burger King in the old Ross Landing building just down the street.

CHAPTER 9

HAWAII AND ALASKA

From the moment your plane touches down and you receive your welcoming "aloha" and flowered lei, you and your grandchild will be hooked on Hawaii. The beauty, the near-perfect weather, the mysteries and paradoxes of these enchanted islands will keep you entranced for as long as you stay and beckon you back as long as you live. A trip to Hawaii is appropriate for children 12 and older.

Getting to Hawaii is easy. Many of the leading airlines offer flights between the mainland and the Hawaiian Islands. It's a five-hour flight from the West Coast. Your travel agent will advise about fares. Be sure to tell him your age and that of your grandchild. It could make a difference in the amount you pay. But any way you look at it, this is not an inexpensive trip.

To avoid an excessively long flight if you are traveling from the east, you may want to fly into Los Angeles or San Francisco a day or so early in order to rest.

Don't forget the time change. You'll be traveling back into yesterday. The islands operate on Hawaiian Standard Time. When it's 2 p.m. on the East Coast, it's 8 a.m. in Hawaii and 11 a.m. on the West Coast. Hawaii does not observe daylight-saving time, so the time difference may increase an hour if where you live is on daylight-saving time.

When you're packing, the name of the game is casual. Sandals or hiking boots if you hike the trails are all you need for footwear. The island kids go barefoot as much as possible, even to school. Your favorite summer casual clothes, a light sweater for evenings and exploring the volcanoes, underthings and at least two swimsuits are basically all you will need.

When you're packing, the name of the game is casual.

Sandals or hiking boots if you hike the trails are

all you need for footwear.

When we think of Hawaii, we usually think of two to five islands. Contrary to popular opinion, though, our 50th state consists of 122 islands stretching over 1,500 miles in the Pacific Ocean. Many of these islands are merely jagged rocks or tiny sandy shoals rising from a great volcanic mountain chain deep in the ocean. It might be great fun to sail along and explore many or all of them, but this may be impractical.

The two best-known and most popular islands are Oahu and Hawaii. Each has its own distinct personality

OAHU

When you go to Hawaii, you'll probably fly into Honolulu International Airport on the island of Oahu. While third in size, Oahu - meaning "gathering place" - is the most densely populated and famous of the islands. It boasts Honolulu, the state's capital city, world-renowned Waikiki Beach and the famous Diamond Head. Pearl Harbor is here also. While the name and place may forever be etched in your memory, it will probably mean nothing to your grandchild.

Whether you rent a car or not, I suggest you stop by one of the car rental counters in the airport and pick up a free "Oahu Drive Guide." It contains a wealth of tourist information. Certainly having a car at your disposal is the best way to see everything at your own pace. Driving in Honolulu is no worse than in any other U.S. city. Rush hours can be frustrating and one-way streets confusing, but not impossible. If you want a rental car, be sure to reserve it well in advance of your arrival. On Oahu, as opposed to some of the other islands, it is possible to use other means of transportation and see the island.

The weather in Hawaii is usually fantastic: balmy and sunny with gorgeous blue skies. The pace of the natives is slow, so it's easy to make this a restful, relaxing vacation. Flexibility is the key to planning your days here. Don't push. Don't rush. Do what you want at as leisurely a pace as you and your grandchild desire. If you want to spend the day at the beach or around the pool, do it. If you want to browse through the shops, hike in the mountains or take a sightseeing tour, do that.

"The Bus" is the island's manmade wonder; it circulates all through Honolulu, into central Oahu and along the north coastline. I believe the best buy in Hawaii is the four-hour, 80-mile trip around the island's Koolan Mountains, including much of the Windward Coast, for 85 cents (correct change only, please). If you have the time, I suggest you take this trip on your first day to orient yourselves to the island and then decide what to do, when and how. Be sure to buy the nominally priced "The Bus Guide" or "Honolulu and Oahu by the Bus." Both are extremely helpful when planning.

A cab ride from the airport to downtown costs approximately $25. Many of the hotels run their own shuttles at a fraction of that cost.

There are tours by boat, bus, van and even submarine ready and waiting for you. Study the brochures in your hotel lobby and don't hesitate to ask questions if there is something you don't understand. One tour likely to appeal to your youngster is led by native islanders and includes an island tour by van, then some boogie boarding (surfing on a small board) and snorkeling (accompanied by certified life guards) from Waimanalo beach. Call True Value Tickets (808) 923-5911 for information and reservations.

Surfing is synonymous with Hawaii. I don't know of any teen or preteen who doesn't want to try it. It is a dangerous sport, though, and even the pros study the swells and the seasons and act accordingly. If your grandchild is as determined to try it as mine was, try the Haleiwa SurfCenter at 66167 Haleiwa Road. Surfing lessons here are free on weekends from April to October when the surf is low.

Waikiki Beach is certainly one of the most famous of all surfing spots in the world and my grandson was eager to try it there. The lessons were very expensive and we were advised that its waves should be avoided by all but the experts. I had to say no.

When you want to go swimming - and you don't want to come to the islands without swimming - stick to beaches where there are lifeguards. But beware, sometimes there are hazardous currents under the gentlest seeming waves. Two beaches that are great for swimming, sunbathing, flying kites and generally having fun are Ala Moana Park and Goat Island off North Shore's Kalanai Point. Sans Souci, across from Kapiolani Park, also has shallow water safe for children.

If you want an oceanside hotel or condominium on Waikiki, expect to pay for it. Prices start at $160 for a double-occupancy room. There are many in the more moderate range only a block or so from the beach and a few in the inexpensive range. Prices are somewhat lower near Diamond Head. Travel agents are invaluable in helping you find something adequate for your needs. They may refer you to a bed-and-breakfast ora group tour if individual plans are beyond your financial reach. Be honest about your price range and other considerations.

Regardless of where you stay, you will want to visit at least one of the larger hotels. At the Royal Hawaiian, often called the "Pink Lady" because of its somewhat garish pink color, you will want to stroll through the wonderful palm gardens down to the prime beachfront. Try to go on Monday for the traditional royal luau at its Coconut Grove. It is by far the best of the luaus and something that must be experienced at least once.

Just down the ocean walk is the Halekulani Hotel built on the site of a 1917 hotel that was the setting for the first of the Charlie Chan detective stories, *The House Without a Key*. You and your young mystery-book lover may want to read this on the plane going over. If you enjoyed *Kidnapped* or *A Child's Garden of Verses*, you will want to visit the fine old Sans Souci and sit and meditate as Robert Louis Stevenson did under a hau tree.

If your grandchild is a teenager, she will probably want to learn the hula. At 10 a.m. on Tuesdays, Wednesdays and Thursdays, the Royal Hawaiian Glee Club puts on a one-hour show ending in a mass class in the hula. It's called the Kodak Hula Show and is in Kapiolani Park. It is usually crowded, so get there early. The doors open at 8:30 a.m.

Also in Kapiolani Park are the Honolulu Zoo and the Waikiki Aquarium, both open daily. The Hawaiian Children's Museum has excellent hands-on science center exhibits that kids love. This is located at Dole Cannery Square. There is a shuttle from the cannery to Waikiki daily.

You may have to wait in line and your youngster may argue about going, but don't miss Pearl Harbor and the Arizona Memorial.

You may have to wait in line and your youngster may argue about going, but don't miss Pearl Harbor and the Arizona Memorial. If your grandchild doesn't know about the morning of Dec. 7, 1941, tell him. If your memory is vague, read up on it or take a sightseeing tour to it. Pearl Harbor is Hawaii's most popular tourist attraction and rightly so. It is open daily, 7:30 to 5. The last program begins at 3.

Next door is the USS Bowfin/Pacific Submarine Museum. It is interesting to anyone who loves submarines. The National Memorial Cemetery of the Pacific - Punchbowl Cemetery - where more than 35,000 American servicemen and women are buried, is very busy on Sundays when visitors come to honor the dead by placing leis and bouquets of flowers on the graves. World War II buffs will want to visit the U.S. Army Museum of Hawaii on Kalia and Saratoga roads. It's open Tuesday through Sunday 10 to 4:15.

Of course, you will have seen the massive Diamond Head looming protectively over the island since you arrived, but to get to it you need to take the road off Monsarat near 18th Avenue, which leads through a tunnel to the floor of the crater. If you are physically up to a hike, take the three-quarters of a mile dirt trail through another tunnel and up a steep 99-step stairway to a gun emplacement. Beyond, three spiral staircases and a steel ladder lead to the crater rim and the most spectacular view of wonderful Waikiki.

THE BIG ISLAND OF HAWAII

The Big Island of Hawaii, as its name implies, is the largest of the islands. Because of the fountains of lava erupting from the two active volcanoes, the island is always increasing in size.

When you visit this island, you fly in to General Lyman Field or Keahole Airport. If you want to visit the black beaches on the Kahala or Kona coasts, you will arrive at the latter. The former provides access to Hilo and Hawaii Volcanoes National Park. If you are on the island for only one day, I suggest you take a Gray Line Tour to the national park.

The guides are well versed in geology, and the vehicles will pick you up at the airport or your hotel. Phone (808) 329-9337 for more information.

The more adventurous of you may want to rent a car and drive about and perhaps do some hiking. Keep in mind that the roads are so often subject to interruption, such as an earthquake, pumice drift or lava flow, that you may find the road suddenly closed. Road crews are always at work reopening them, but driving can be uncertain. If you choose to drive, take Highway 11 from the airport to Hilo in the park. It is a breathtakingly beautiful and interesting drive. The 11-mile Crater Rim Drive around the Kilauea Caldera is also. Legend has it that Pele, fire goddess, makes her home at the rim of Halemalumalu Crater within the Kilauea Caldera. You will see bouquets of flowers, leis, fruit, food and drink left on the rim as offerings to Pele, who remains a popular and respected pagan goddess.

If you are on the island for only one day,

I suggest you take a Gray Line Tour to

the national park.

Seeing the lava flows and tubes, the volcanic ash, the pahochoes, the pumice drift - often with curtains of fire and rivers of hot lava - is certainly reason enough to visit this ever-changing island. Be sure to stop at Thurston Lava Tube and walk through this old volcanic cave.

If you have a second day in the park, drive down the Chain of Craters Road, where lava is usually flowing to the sea. Trails both long and short abound and are wonderful, out-of-this-world experiences. Always stay on marked roads and trails and obey signs regarding closings and detours. For current updates of volcanic activity, keep your car radio tuned to AM 530.

Another popular way to see the island is to take an aerial tour. There are several departing from Lyman Field in Hilo.

Regardless of the number of islands you visit, whether it is one or more, you surely will fall in love with our 50th state. The

beauty, the relaxed atmosphere and the friendliness of the islanders make Hawaii an ideal place for an intergenerational vacation.

ALASKA

Any way you look at it, getting to Alaska is costly. So if you
are budget conscious, you will want to check out the various
means of transportation before deciding how to go. Certainly
the most popular and easiest way is to book a cruise-tour. A
luxury ship will glide you up the Inside Passage through the
most spectacular natural scenery you and your grandchild
will ever see. Since a steady diet of looking at beautiful, snow-
covered mountains and icy glaciers may not be big on many
youngsters' agendas, make sure before you book your cruise
that your ship has special activities planned for your grandchild's age group. If he is occupied and happy, you can sit
back and enjoy your activities.

There will be several ports of call with time to disembark and
tour along the way, including Juneau, Alaska's capital and the
nearest port to the famous Mendenhall Glacier.

At Anchorage, you likely will have a choice of several land or
air tours. I suggest you choose the glass-topped train trip to
Denali National Park to see the massive Denali and the Arctic
wildlife, to say nothing of the grand and magnificent interior
of this great state.

Other, less-expensive ways to get to our 49th state include
driving the 1,523-mile Alaska Highway from Dawson Creek
in British Columbia, Canada, to Fairbanks. Unless your grandchildren are older, capable of automotive repair and able to
take care of you, I wouldn't recommend it.

You may opt to fly to Anchorage or Fairbanks from the Lower
48 and take bus, rail or plane trips from there. Check the
prices before you leave, not only for the tours of choice but
also for lodging and meals. You may find that a cruise is a
better buy. This is likely to be true if you take the ferry up the
Inside Passage departing from Prince Rupert, B.C., Canada.

This is a much less costly and less luxurious way to see the same fantastic scenery. Reservations for this kind of trip must be made months in advance. For information call the Alaska Marine Highway toll-free at (888) 256-6784.

Regardless of the way you choose to go, be sure to do extensive research on what you and your grandchild want to see and do when you get to Alaska. There are so many choices, many with great appeal, that you easily could overextend your budget and your energy before you've seen your top priorities.

CHAPTER 10

NEW YORK

New York City is the most exciting city in America. It is a smorgasbord of culture, history, sports, recreation and fun. No matter where your grandchild's primary interests lie, the Big Apple can satisfy the child's appetite. New York City is appropriate for a visit by children 12 and older.

Extensive planning is essential. The two of you need to sit down together, study your tourist materials, set priorities and make decisions about what you want to see and do. Check the Sunday edition of *The New York Times* (most public libraries have it) to see what special events, sports activities, plays, concerts and other events are planned for when you intend to be there.

I definitely do not recommend driving in New York City unless you have done it before and are comfortable with the traffic. Even then, don't go in during rush hours. Keep in mind that most avenues are one way north or south, while numbered streets are all one way, with even-numbered street usually eastbound and odd-numbered westbound.

Very likely you will fly into the LaGuardia, Kennedy or Newark airport. Taxis from any of the airports to midtown Manhattan are quite expensive. I suggest you take one of the express buses from the airport to the Port Authority Bus Terminal at West 42nd Street and Eighth Avenue. From there, you can take a taxi to your hotel at a far more reasonable price.

There are an abundance of good hotels in Manhattan. They are so well located - many within walking distance of theaters, museums and restaurants - that it will be worth the cost. Remember when you call for reservations to ask for any discounts that might be available to you. When deciding on a hotel, take into consideration the special events you will want to see. For example, if you have a young drama lover, be aware that most Broadway theaters are located just east or west of Broadway between 41st and 53rd streets.

There are an abundance of good hotels in Manhattan. They are so well located - many within walking distance of theaters, museums and restaurants - that it will be worth the cost.

Music lovers and dance enthusiasts will undoubtedly want to attend events at Lincoln Center for the Performing Arts, located at Broadway and 65th Street. Budding artists will want to start their museum trek with the huge and wonderful Metropolitan Museum of Art at Fifth Avenue at 82nd Street.

Sports fans may choose to be near Madison Square Garden, where the Knicks play basketball and the Rangers play hockey. This is located between Seventh and Eighth avenues and 31st and 33rd streets.

After you check in to your hotel, go outside and walk down the canyon-like street, looking up at the massive skyscrapers. It is an experience like no other, especially if this is your first trip to New York City. On subsequent trips, these vertical monsters will seem to shrink somewhat in height.

As usual, a sightseeing bus tour should be on the agenda for your first full day. There are innumerable tours ranging from about two hours to all day. You may want to select an all-day tour or shorter ones that encompass much that you want to see. There are special bus tours now that take you all around the city, stopping at various locations such as Greenwich Village (a must for teens) and museum mile. You pay one fee and can hop on and off the bus at designated locations as often as you wish. Ask at your hotel desk for information about the various tours.

In general, children and grown-ups love New York City. It is different, vibrant and exciting. There is so much to see and do, to experience and savor.

In general, children and grown-ups love New York City. It is different, vibrant and exciting. There is so much to see and do, to experience and savor. You can't do it all in a week or a month or even a year, but you can have an unforgettable experience.

Places that I've visited with my grandchildren and have particularly enjoyed include taking the elevator to the 86th floor of the Empire State Building and going out on the glass-enclosed observation deck for a fantastic view of the city.

The Statue of Liberty is also a must. If your city tour did not include a boat trip out to this landmark, you can take the ferry from Battery Park in Lower Manhattan daily from 9:30 to 3:30. Return trips are every 30 minutes. If your family came to this country through nearby Ellis Island, you can combine a visit there with your trip to the Statue of Liberty. You'll enjoy this vast, rather intimidating building - now restored for the public's enjoyment with exhibits and gift shop. The names of many immigrants are engraved on plaques outside the building.

Speaking of ferry rides, a trip on the Staten Island Ferry gives you a wonderful view of Lower Manhattan and the round trip fare is only 50 cents (quarters only). Where else can you find such a bargain? But do avoid the commuter rush hours.

Radio City Music Hall is something to be remembered forever. The chandeliers here are some of the the world's largest. The theater is enormous and the stairway looks as if it came directly from a royal palace in Europe. Guided tours from the lobby are every half hour from 10 to 5 Monday through Saturday and from 11 to 5 on Sunday. The stage shows, featuring the world-famous Rockettes, are always a treat for youngsters, especially if you have a granddaughter. You might find her kicking her heels high after seeing this show.

Adjacent to Rockefeller Center in the G.E. building are the NBC television network offices. NBC Studio Tours are conducted Monday through Friday 8:30 to 5:30. If you're up early you may want to join the group of eager fans outside during the morning *Today* show. It's traditional for the hosts to come out and talk to the street audience periodically throughout the two-hour show.

If shopping is on your agenda, don't overlook Macy's, reputed to be the world's largest department store, or Bloomingdale's, Manhattan's most famous.

The Bronx Zoo, at 265 acres, is the largest urban zoo in the United States. It includes a Wild Asia exhibit where elephants, tigers and other such animals roam relatively free through a 40-acre wilderness. They can be seen from the monorail. Congo Gorilla Forest is home to two troops of lowland gorillas plus mandrills, monkeys, okapi and other wildlife.

The American Museum of Natural History is a joy to all ages. The largest blue sapphire ever found is on display in the Hall of Gems and Minerals.

Want to try ice-skating? The Rockefeller Plaza Rink and the Wollman Memorial Rink in Central Park are open in the winter.

The huge, pastoral patch of green in the middle of New York's sea of steel and brownstone is famous Central Park. It is here that Shakespeare reigns supreme - and free - in the summer outdoor theater. You can also attend a free performance of the New York Philharmonic here in the summer. There's also a lake with boat rentals, bicycle trails, restaurants and jogging paths. But be warned: Central Park is fine to visit in the daylight hours, but positively should never be entered at night.

Theater tickets, which are expensive, are available for many shows at a discount if you're willing to wait until the day of the performance and stand in line at the TKTS booth in Times Square. For evening performances, the booths are open Monday through Saturday from 3 to 8 p.m. and 10 to 2 for Wednesday and Saturday matinees. Only cash or traveler's checks are accepted.

Whether you enjoy the flickering lights

of the soaring midtown skyscrapers, the hustle

and bustle of rush hour, the ethnic neighborhoods like

Chinatown and Little Italy, or the enjoyment of music,

dance and theater, you surely will be entranced by

this sensational city. It was a visit my grandson

Philip and I will forever treasure,

and so will you.

Tickets to the major television shows can be obtained usually by mail. You'll find more information on how to get tickets by visiting the individual websites of the networks: abc.go.com, cbs.com and nbc.com. The sites will have details about the individual show you want to see.

If you and your grandchild enjoy walking, you might want to try some of the various guided walking tours sponsored by

the Municipal Art Society. Call the society at (212) 935-3960.
You can contact the Museum of the City of New York at (212)
534-1672, or the Big Onion Walking Tours at (212) 439-1090.

Whether you enjoy the flickering lights of the soaring midtown skyscrapers, the hustle and bustle of rush hour, the ethnic neighborhoods like Chinatown and Little Italy, or the
enjoyment of music, dance and theater, you surely will be
entranced by this sensational city. It was a visit my grandson
Philip and I will forever treasure, and so will you.

UPSTATE NEW YORK

In upstate New York on the Canadian border is Niagara Falls.
The best view from the American side is the Observation
Tower at Prospect Point or at its base. On the Canadian side, it
is Queen Victoria Park. I strongly suggest that you view the
Falls from both points. If you are there for only one day and
you don't want to drive across the International Bridge into
Canada, you can take either the Bedore U.S. and Canadian
Boat and Van Tour. The Bedore Tour leaves from the Howard
Johnson at the Falls as well as from other hotels in the down-
town area, and includes the *Maid of the Mist* boat trip, an abso-
lute must for all ages.

If you plan to spend the night at Niagara, my recommenda-
tion is to stay on the Canadian side within easy walking distance of the Falls so you can take in the impressive nightly
illumination of this natural wonder.

CHAPTER 11

THE SOUTHWEST

I f you live in the East, you're in for a treat just seeing the varied topography of the Southwest United States. It is so beautiful with its deserts, mountains, canyons and forests. Visiting this area is most appropriate with your grandchildren ages 10 and up.

The more interesting spots for intergenerational exploring lie in the northern section of Arizona in the vicinity of Flagstaff. I suggest you fly into Arizona's capital city of Phoenix, rent a car and drive north 200 miles to the Grand Canyon, or arrange for a connecting flight from Phoenix to Flagstaff. Amtrak trains stop regularly in the middle of Flagstaff as do Greyhound buses. Although there are Gray Line tours and scenic flights to several of the nearby points of interest, having a car at your disposal will be an enormous convenience and give you a great deal more flexibility - which is important, especially when traveling with the younger generation.

As you leave Phoenix, take Interstate 17 north. After about 90 miles, plan to stop at Montezuma Castle National Monument. It contains ruins of an ancient cliff dwelling built in the 12th or 13th century. The five-story castle is believed to have been inhabited by Indians. Other ruins dot the nearby cliffs. A self-guiding trail has excellent views of the area. My granddaughter was fascinated and we spent more time there than we had planned. There is a picnic area if you prepare a take-along lunch. We were not prepared, but wished we had been as there weren't many roadside eateries available.

Seeing the Grand Canyon is undoubtedly your primary reason for this trip, but there are other places of interest in the area that you should consider if you have the time.

When you have found a motel in Flagstaff, before or after you visit the Grand Canyon, take a day trip north on I-40, first to the Meteor Crater and then on to the Petrified Forest and Painted Desert. Meteor Crater is a huge hole blasted by a meteorite 50,000 years ago. Located six miles south of I-40 on a well-marked road, it is about 38 miles east of Flagstaff. While you can't hike into the crater, you can see it, listen to the audio presentation and read about it. It's fascinating.

Traveling east about 20 miles past Holbrook, you come to the Petrified Forest National Park, where erosion is unearthing a fossilized prehistoric forest of brilliantly colored, gigantic trees lying broken over the ground. Near the south entrance is the Long Log Trail, where you get a good view of bright stone logs. Numerous fossil bones and plants have been found in the park, giving rise to the theory that the early dinosaurs once roamed this area.

A scenic 28-mile drive runs through the park, which is open 8 to 5 daily. Near the northern entrance, you can see the Painted Desert, a vast expanse of sand dunes, which take on different colors at different times of the day. Rather than retracing your steps, I suggest you enter at the north entrance from I-40 and exit at the south gate, which will put you on Highway 180, 18 miles southeast of Holbrook. Go back to Holbrook and take I-40 west to return to Flagstaff.

Keep in mind that it is illegal to collect plants, rocks, sand or pieces of petrified wood inside the park. Violators can incur heavy fines and sometimes prison. The gift shops in the area sell a variety of specimens collected from private areas outside the park, so wait and buy your souvenirs there.

If you are a hiker, another interesting day would be to take Highway 89 about 12 miles north of Flagstaff to go to Volcano National Monument Sunset Crater, one of the many volcanoes in the San Francisco Volcanic Field. There are many trails leading into the San Francisco peaks. Even if you aren't a walker, you can take the chairlift from the Arizona Snowbowl almost to the top of Mount Agassiz -12,350 feet high - for spectacular views.

For those looking for a more strenuous walk, try the Walnut Canyon National Monument located about 10 miles east of Flagstaff off I-40. It has steep steps leading down to the visitor center.

Now for the pièce de résistance - the Grand Canyon of the Colorado River, certainly one of our national treasures. Only 85 miles north of Flagstaff via I-40, then west to Williams and Highway 64 north is the South Rim of the Canyon. Very likely this will be your destination, because it is easier to get to than the North Rim and has far more tourist facilities. Also, it is open all year.

If possible, make your reservations well in advance

and try to stay in one of the picturesque old

hotels on the rim inside the park.

The views from the two rims differ considerably. Both are extremely interesting and you might want to visit both. From the Grand Canyon Village at the South Rim, it is 214 miles to the Grand Canyon Lodge on the North Rim. This scenic drive passes through a portion of the Navajo Reservation, the Painted Desert, Kaibab National Forest and over the Navajo Bridge at the northeast end of the park. An engineering masterpiece, this bridge is 616 feet long and 467 feet high.

Assuming that you go to the South Rim as we did, you will find a variety of motels in Tusayan, nine miles south of Grand Canyon Village, and even more just outside the entrance to the park.

If possible, make your reservations well in advance and try to stay in one of the picturesque old hotels on the rim inside the park. For accommodation reservations in the park, write Grand Canyon National Park Lodges, P.O. Box 699, Grand Canyon National Park, AZ 86023, call (928) 638-2401 or contact your travel agent.

In case you haven't visited the Grand Canyon in some years, you will find changes. Passenger cars are no longer allowed on the West Rim Drive during the summer. Free shuttle service is available along this drive from March through November. Sightseeing buses offering a variety of tours depart from the lodges within the park.

I recommend the Combination Tour, which lasts six hours and costs $33 for adults; children are free. It has an excellent narrated tour. For schedules and reservations, call the Bright Angel Transportation Desk at (928) 638-3283.

At sunset, regardless of where you stay, you must walk out to Hopi Point and the Bright Angel Trail as it winds across the Tonto Platform to see the shadows magically changing the vistas. The best place to watch the sunrise is Mather Point, some distance north of the visitor center. No matter where you are or what time of day it is, the views are magnificent.

Helicopter and airplane tours of the canyon leave Grand Canyon Airport in Tusayan throughout the day. Also in Tusayan is the Grand Canyon IMAX Theater, which presents an informative film called *Grand Canyon - The Hidden Secrets*.

For intergenerational travel, I really do not recommend the one-day mule trips that go down to the canyon floor, although I am sure your grandchild would opt for it in a second. However, if you are in excellent physical shape and very brave, it would be a memorable trip. You might want to spend the night at the Phantom Ranch if you decide to go. Reservations for this, of course, need to be made well in advance.

Back toward Phoenix, you may want to take Highway 89A south from Flagstaff through Red Rock Country and Oak

Creek Canyon. This canyon certainly can't compare with the Grand Canyon, but its sheer walls are vividly striped with color and, more important, you can drive through it. Slide Rock State Park near there is a natural water chute where you can swim and slide across large, smooth rocks in the middle of the river - no doubt a great joy to your traveling companion if not to you.

At Sedona you will probably turn east and pick up I-17 south into Phoenix for your return home. As our airplane waited its turn to taxi down the runway, I turned to my 10-year-old granddaughter. "What did you think?" I asked. "Awesome," was her only comment. What more could you ask?

As our airplane waited its turn to taxi down the runway,

I turned to my 10-year-old granddaughter.

"What did you think?" I asked.

"Awesome," was her only comment.

What more could you ask?

Carlsbad Caverns National Park

Far south in the southwest corner of New Mexico is Carlsbad Caverns National Park. Too amazing a geological spectacle to miss if at all possible, its nearest city is El Paso, Texas.

Carlsbad Caverns are open every summer day. Your grandchild might enjoy the nightly exiting of tons of thousands of bats that make their home hanging upside down from the ceiling of the cave. At about dusk, black clouds of these small creatures fly out of the mouth of the cave and spread out for miles searching for food. It is a phenomenon you definitely do not want to miss. Park rangers are present to answer questions and give you information.

Sometimes, but not often, grannies can be dull and just down-right boring. On one particularly long drive, Katie saved the day. "Granny," she suddenly announced, "I guess you didn't know it, but today is Wrinkles' birthday and he has to have a party.

Wrinkles is Katie's stuffed dog, without whom she refuses to travel. It was as if the sun had come out from behind a cloud. We spent the remainder of the drive planning activities and food for Wrinkles' party. It was a huge success.

We swam with Wrinkles playing lifeguard. We toured the motel property showing everything to Wrinkles. He met the desk clerk and one of the housekeepers. We chose our dinner menu from the snack machines - sodas, peanut butter and cheese crackers, peanuts and candy bars - and ended the evening with Wrinkles propped up on the bed beside his devoted Katie watching cartoons.

Even now, years later, when things get a little slow, Katie is prone to announce, "It's Wrinkles' birthday."

" Granny," she suddenly announced, "I guess you didn't know it, but today is Wrinkles' birthday and he has to have a party. "

So remember, it's the experience, not the destination that's important. With that said, I recognize that every section of this great nation of ours has a multitude of opportunities for wonderful intergenerational travel. Some may be so close to your home that you haven't considered them. Others may seem to be too far away.

OKLAHOMA

Whether the blood of the American Indian flows through your veins or you and your grandchild are fascinated by Native American lore, Oklahoma is a state you won't want to miss.

Anadarko, southwest of Oklahoma City, is the center of what once was the hunting grounds for several of the local Delaware, Kiowa, Wichita and Caddo Indian tribes. It is now the home of the Bureau of Indian Affairs serving western Oklahoma and hosts a weeklong American Indian Exposition each August. Here, too, are the Anadarko Philomathic Museum, Indian City USA, which is a re-creation of a Plains Indian village, the National Hall of Fame for Famous American Indians and the Southern Plains Indian Museum and Crafts Center.

About five miles north of Lawton is the Fort Sill Military Reservation and National Historic Landmark. You can see the Geronimo Guardhouse here and visit the graves of several famous Indians including Geronimo on Chief's Knoll in the Old Post Cemetery. There are authentic relics commemorating the American Indian on the grounds of the museum.

The Cherokee National Holiday during the weekend before Labor Day is celebrated in Tahlequah. While here, don't miss the "Trail of Tears" outdoor drama, which tells the sad story of the forced march of Cherokee Indians from the Smoky Mountains in North Carolina to Oklahoma. Tishomingo was the capital of the Chickasaw Nation. The restored council house stands on Court House square.

Wherever you are in this state, you can't miss the influence of the American Indian whether it is in the name of the town or the abundance of museums and historic galleries. So, go, enjoy and learn.

TEXAS

With more than one teenager in tow, head for San Antonio and its famed Paseo del Rio - Riverwalk.

Make sure you have reservations in a hotel *on* the Riverwalk. Then you can sit back, relax and allow your grandchildren the privilege of branching out on their own - providing, of course, that you can trust them not to leave the Riverwalk area and be back by a certain time.

The three-mile walk along the tree-shaded San Antonio River is well lighted, busy with pedestrians and boat traffic and safer than any tourist area I've seen for youngsters to be on their own. Be sure, though that there are two or more of them and they stay together. At the end of Riverwalk is the fabulous River Center Mall, a delight for any teenage shopper with its 125 stores and restaurants. This is where they will spend most of their time - as long as you allow.

During June and August, musical events are performed in the Arneson River Theatre. This is an outdoor amphitheater that has tiered seats on one side of the river and the stage on the other. The productions are even more fun because of the river taxis and the passing boats that float down between them.

Before you leave San Antonio, be sure to visit The Alamo if for no other reason than for your youngsters to be able to say "been there, done that."

CHAPTER 12

CRUISING, CAMPING, VISITING A DUDE RANCH AND SEARCHING FOR YOUR FAMILY'S ROOTS

When you travel with two or more grandchildren, you may want to consider either a cruise or a dude ranch, provided, that is, they offer enough activities to keep your little ones interested when they tire of you and vice versa. If the prices seem too high initially, consider that they include almost everything: transportation, food and entertainment. It also leaves time for you to do things that appeal to you, even if it's only relaxing on deck or under a tree with a good book, without feeling guilty.

CRUISING

Check with a travel agent you trust. Ask around and find one who specializes in cruises and knows which cruise line offers what. Not all of them will meet your needs. After you have determined how much you want to spend and what type of cruise your money will buy, start with questions such as:

✔ What programs are there for what ages? If it's only sitting down and coloring all day, forget it.

✔ What are the youngest and oldest ages for participation? What are the age divisions? Nine-year-old Johnny won't go if 3-year-old Jean is in the same place.

✔ How many counselors are there for how many children?

✔ Is there a library with children's books?

✔ How much space is reserved for the children's activities?

✔ Is individual baby-sitting available if Granny wants an evening of adult activities?

✔ Are pizzas, burgers and ice cream available throughout the day?

✔ Are there special menu choices for children in the main dining room?

✔ Is there a children's pool?

✔ Are there special hours for children in the main pools?

✔ Are swimming or snorkeling lessons available?

✔ Is there a special movie theater for the kids? Or will there be appropriate films shown at special times?

✔ Are there toys and games that can be checked out overnight?

If you find a cruise that you and your grandchildren want to take, consider it for an entire family reunion in the future. This can be a very special treat for all grandparents, adult children and grandchildren.

A couple of Christmases ago, I splurged and took the entire family - children, spouses and grandchildren - on a weeklong

Caribbean cruise. It was wonderful. There were age-appropriate activities for the grandchildren, leaving their parents with some much-appreciated time on their own. I got my motherly and grandmotherly fix by spending individual and group time with my children and grandchildren. We all had dinner together each evening, but the rest of the time everyone did as they pleased.

Nobody had to do a thing - not make a bed, wash a dish or prepare a meal. All we had to do was sit back, enjoy and make a memory. And, believe me, we did.

It was expensive, yes. And certainly not something many of us could afford very often. But by the time I figured in all the costs of preparing the house for guests, decorating, purchasing holiday food and gifts and providing entertainment for several days, I'm not sure I would have saved all that much. Besides, nobody had to do a thing - not make a bed, wash a dish or prepare a meal. All we had to do was sit back, enjoy and make a memory. And, believe me, we did.

CAMPING

Years ago when our children were youngsters and many of our friends were extolling the virtues of camping, we decided to try it. A trip to Sears found us several hundred dollars poorer, but the proud possessors of camping equipment - seven sleeping bags, seven air mattresses, a tent to sleep five kids and two adults, a Coleman stove, coolers and a variety of small but necessary (according to the salesman) items. We were ready. The kids were thrilled!

Our first - and only - trip was to a much-touted lakeside state park 150 miles from home. We arrived in the middle of afternoon and pitched the tent - a difficult but not impossible task. While their father took the children swimming, I prepared our gourmet first-camping-experience dinner. By nightfall we were all exhausted and zipped ourselves into the sleeping bags. I was just getting comfortable when a small voice piped up, "I have to go to the bathroom."

That began what seemed to be an endless parade to the bathhouse 150 yards from our campsite. Finally, after what seemed like an eternity, everyone settled down and one by one drifted off to sleep. In the middle of the night, loud rolls of thunder awakened us. Bright flashes of lightning illuminated our tent. Then the rain started, pelting hard on the canvas overhead. After huddling together for some moments, my husband said, "This is it."

He braved the storm and backed up the station wagon to the tent door. I handed the children to him one by one and he virtually threw them into the back of the car. Then he and I jumped into the front seat and took off to the warmth and comfort of a Holiday Inn in a nearby town. Thus ended our camping experience by group consensus. Not so for many of you, I know.

If you're among the multitudes of campers, whether in a modern recreational vehicle, a pop-up trailer or a tent, there's no reason not to enjoy it with your grandchildren. The minimum age for grandchildren, I'm told, should be 7 or 8 because there are jobs for everyone in setting up camp. If you're planning a trip to Alaska, up the minimum age of 17. A preview of these responsibilities and the grandparent's rules and expectations should be gone over thoroughly before you and your grandchild leave home.

Single grandparents are not excluded from this experience, although you may want to increase the minimum age of your youngsters to 10 or 12. If you have any problems, you'll find eager-to-help next-door campers ready and willing, so you need never feel alone.

Another suggestion my friends make is to travel with two or more grandchildren at a time. While this limits the one-on-one relationship with your grandchild, a different type of bonding takes place. The kids not only buddy with each other, they also branch out at the campground to meet other youngsters and families from all over the country. It can foster independence as well as teach responsibility under the guidance of loving grandparents.

Camping spaces are small and camping families universally friendly. Often, lasting friendships between adults and children are made in a very short time. It is not unusual to meet two or more families who continue to keep in touch - and even travel together - through the years. Youngsters often become pen pals and, in one instance I recall, two boys visited each other's homes for years and later became college roommates.

Throughout this country and Canada are many excellent campgrounds. Most campers I have interviewed choose the national parks and state parks, followed by the well-known parks such as KOA. Most campgrounds have very good bathhouses, hook-ups for electricity and playgrounds, swimming pools, rental boats and other activities All will gladly furnish you with informational material.

You may want to check out the website of the area you plan to visit. AAA has CampBook guides available without charge to members. Planning is as important here as it is in the any other trip. Keep in mind that Golden Age Passports are good for a 50 percent discount on user fees at federally operated campgrounds. Remember, though, these passports can't be issued by mail. You must appear in person to obtain them.

Some grandparent-campers like to select an area of interest and stay there - enjoying the swimming, boating, fishing, hiking or whatever the area affords. It is easier, they say, to do this than to pack up each day and move on. They feel it is more relaxing for them and gives the grandchildren a better chance to make friends and truly enjoy being together.

Others, however, take an entirely different tack. They are tourists by nature and prefer the nomadic life even if it requires a little more planning and work. It isn't unusual for them to take a summer and travel all across the country, seeing and sharing with their grandchildren the many wonders our nation has. Often, they may pull their family car behind their RV to use when touring large cities and the outlying areas.

> **66** **It isn't unusual for them to take a summer and travel all across the country, seeing and sharing with their grandchildren the many wonders our nation has. 99**

As with any type of travel, you can make it as expensive as you choose. RVs are gas-guzzlers. Towing a car, of course, lets you save money because you don't have to drive the RV everywhere. Pulling pop-up trailers certainly requires more gas than just driving the family car, but usually gets better mileage than an RV. Fees at campgrounds are less than motel prices, and you have the advantage of preparing your own meals, which may cut your costs considerably.

If you are making a decision about whether to camp solely in order to save money, study the situation carefully. Know your habits and what you want from a vacation. Do you choose to prepare most of your meals in camp? How far do you plan to travel? What is your timeframe? Do you want to do extensive touring or stay close to camp? What are the ages of the grandchildren you plan to take? How much help can you expect from them? What are your own physical capabilities or limitations? Are you a veteran camper? Do you love the camping experience and truly want to share it with your grandchildren?

If you are a couple or a single grandparent who loves camping, go for it. One widowed grandmother I know said that she never feels safer than when camping with her grandchildren. There is a camaraderie between campers that you don't find elsewhere. If this is your experience, then by all means extend it to include your grandchildren. Happy camping!

> 66 Your trip could be as short as around your hometown if you, your parents, your children and grandchildren were born and still live in the same town. 99

VISITING A DUDE RANCH

Dude ranches, like cruises, can be the ideal spot for a family reunion, especially if yours is an outdoor family. There are activities for everyone, no matter how many of you there are. So pack up your cowboy gear - boots are an absolute must - and head west.

Although dude ranches have a great appeal for youngsters 6 and older, teenagers seem to like them best. Many ranches have special teen counselors to take the kids on all-day outings. Being with your own age group is so important when a youngster is in this in-between stage. The fact that you are willing to pay for a vacation and not insist that they spend every waking hour with you will greatly endear you to them. Be ready and eager to hear anything they want to share about their day. Listening is an art at which grandparents excel and being heard is something adolescents need so much.

There are dozens of ranches available. Check with a travel agent who has experience in booking such vacations, or visit the library or cruise the Internet, then call the ranches directly until you are satisfied with your choice.

SEARCHING FOR YOUR FAMILY'S ROOTS

Perhaps the best of all intergenerational trips is a heritage tour, which helps your grandchildren discover their roots. Seeing the places where parents, grandparents and even great-grandparents lived, attended school and worked is of great interest, even to young children.

Your trip could be as short as around your hometown if you, your parents, your children and grandchildren were born and still live in the same town. Unless you live in the same house, a trip to where great-grandpa was born, even if the house is no longer there, is a good place to start the tour, take a picture and begin a scrapbook. Continue through the other members of the family. You may want to use a video camera to record different places and remember to tell stories about the person you're "visiting" as you go.

Or your tour may take you across the state, the country or even abroad. You may take different grandchildren at different times or several at a time. It may not be possible to complete such a tour in one trip or even two. It may even take several years, but it will be a wonderful family memoir and one that will live forever.

CHAPTER 13

CANADA

I s your granddaughter enamored with Anne of Green Gables? Do you have a grandson or granddaughter beginning to study French in school? Or one who is fascinated with everything British? If so, perhaps it is time to introduce them to a foreign country without even crossing an ocean. A visit to our northern neighbor is appropriate with children 10 and older.

When you visit outside of the United States, there are a few things you need to keep in mind. First, at the border you will need proof of citizenship for yourself and your grandchild. This may be in the form of a birth or baptismal certificate and photo ID for your youngster, and birth certificate and voter registration card for you, but I recommend passports for each of you. Although not required for travel to Canada, they are easier to handle and are the best identification you can have anywhere in the world. Besides, you will have them for future international travel.

Be sure to carry with you at all time the notarized parental statement with an additional statement giving you permission to travel outside the United States with your grandchild.

Sometimes you can breeze through customs with no questions asked. Or it may not be so easy. Friends of mine were held for about 24 hours once while the border agents tried to reach their grandchild's parents for their permission to take him out of the country. Unfortunately, the parents were out of town and difficult to reach, so my friends' vacation was on hold until the parents were found.

Your driver's license is valid in Canada, but be certain it isn't about to expire. Also call your insurance agent and request and bring with you a Canadian nonresident Inter-Provincial Motor Vehicle Liability card. Also, you need to carry your car registration or, in case of a rental car, your contract.

Be sure to carry with you at all time the notarized parental statement with an additional statement giving you permission to travel outside the United States with your grandchild.

Summer temperatures tend to be a little cooler in Canada than in the States, so don't forget to pack a jacket and some heavy clothing for each of you. You will, of course, carry your cellular phone. Be aware, however, that except in large cities, zero (not 911) is the emergency number.

When making your hotel reservations, be sure to tell them you are a member of AAA. The Canadian Automobile Association honors AAA membership.

Canadian police request that you drive with your headlights on low beam even in daylight.

Speed limits and distances are measured in kilometers. Let your grandchild figure it for you in miles (kilometers times .6 and add 2). For example, 100 kilometers = 62 miles. It is fun for him and great math practice, too.

PRINCE EDWARD ISLAND
Likely your granddaughter's love for Lucy Maude Montgomery's *Anne of Green Gables* series is the reason for being here, so please warn her ahead of time that this is the home of the author and the fictional home of Anne. Many of the places she will see are described in the books, but few scenes for the

movies were filmed here. Most were filmed in a Toronto movie studio. This came as a shock and disappointment to my granddaughter and it took a while for her to relax and enjoy the visit.

Lucy Maude Montgomery and her fictional Anne are synonymous with Prince Edward Island, and you will find reminders throughout the island. Green Gables House, immortalized in the books (with some external shots in the films) is in Cavandish and is part of Prince Edward Island National Park. It was partially destroyed by fire in 1997, but has been restored and is again open for visitors.

Also in Cavandish is the site of the author's home. While the old farmhouse and outbuildings no longer exist, it is where Lucy Maude spent her childhood when she came to live with her grandparents.

Rainbow Valley, on Highway 6 just outside of Cavandish, contains Anne of Green Gables Land, a children's playground and an amusement park with water slides and boats for rent.

From late June to September, the musical production *Anne of Green Gables* is presented in the Confederation Centre of the Arts in Charlottetown. The gallery contains original handwritten manuscripts of Lucy Maude Montgomery's works.

Double-decker sightseeing buses leave the Confederation Centre daily at 10:30 a.m. for a seven-hour Anne of Green Gables Tour. The Anne of Green Gables Museum at Silver Bush Home is located near Park Corner on Prince Edward Island. Lucy Maude's birthplace near New London is open daily from the middle of May to September. Her burial place is in the Cavandish cemetery. You also will find motels, bed-and-breakfasts and restaurants named for the island's most famous author and her heroine.

In case you or your granddaughter tire of Anne and Lucy Maude, you might like to try deep-sea fishing. Even if you never wanted to fish, I think you will enjoy it here, mainly because it is so inexpensive. For $15 for adults, and less for youngsters, you can go out on three-hour charters from the many ports along the North Shore. My granddaughter and I did this more than once. She always brought in her limit of haddock in a very short time. I was a little slower, but caught an eel and a tuna on one trip and a variety of fish on the others. We found that the morning charter is better because the fish are hungry.

If your grandchildren haven't sampled lobster, let them try it here, where it is wonderful and inexpensive. St. Ann's Church at Hope River, New Glasgow Lobster Suppers and the Fisherman's Wharf Lobster Supper in North Rustico are our favorites.

The island's finest sand beaches lie between Souris and Bothwell. Keep in mind, though, that this water is usually colder than what you're accustomed to - after all, it is the North Atlantic. Because Prince Edward Island is small and flat, bicycling is a favorite sport. Rental bikes are available almost everywhere. It's great fun to tour this island of green pastures and rustic villages in this way.

Despite my granddaughter's disappointment in not seeing all the places shown in the *Anne* films, she fell in love with the island and longs to return. The *Anne* musical and the deep-sea fishing were unquestionably the high points of the trip for her.

QUEBEC
Although English is the primary language in Canada, the province of Quebec is the exception. Here French is the number one language with English as a second. Visiting the province of Quebec is appropriate with a grandchild age 14 and older.

If your grandchild is studying French in school, this is a wonderful opportunity for him to practice. Regardless of your linguistic skills, relax and let him speak for you. For both your sakes, though, I suggest each of you carry a pocket English-French dictionary. You will find menus in most restaurants in large cities printed in both languages. Not so in the country, though, where your dictionary and knowledge will come in handy.

If your grandchild is studying French in school, this is a wonderful opportunity for him to practice. Regardless of your linguistic skills, relax and let him speak for you.

We stopped for breakfast one morning in a small roadside restaurant between Montreal and Quebec City. The hand-printed menu was in French only. My grandson thought he was ordering cereal with blueberries, but got dry toast and a glass of juice. I fared little better - I got coffee, which I ordered, and a hard roll, which I did not.

Most shops, even the smaller ones, have at least one bilingual clerk. And if they don't, pantomiming with smiles usually will get you what you want. Getting the wrong thing and being confused is part of the fun and will give you and your grandchild many laughs for a long time to come.

I suggest you plan your vacation in the Old World city of Quebec. It is so Parisian in atmosphere that it is hard to believe it is on this side of the Atlantic. Perched precariously on a high cliff over the St. Lawrence River, the old walled city with its narrow cobbled streets, tiny boutiques, outdoor artists' displays, restaurants and *pensiones* is truly fascinating. Towering like a jewel in a royal crown over Old Quebec is the famed Chateau Frontenac. Whether you choose to stay here or not, be sure to take a tour of its massive lobbies. If your budget allows a stay here, your grandchild will be thrilled because it is so large, so castle-like and so mysterious.

After a night here, you may want to find lodgings in one of the many charming little inns, or *pensiones*, on the streets, or *rues*, surrounding the chateau for the remainder of your stay. You'll save money, yes, but they are so very European and no less interesting. I predict that you and your grandchild will love them. While it is wise to have advance reservations, you may be able to walk the area and find a room at the last minute.

The two best ways to tour the historic Upper Town of Old Quebec City is on foot and by horse-drawn carriage, or *calèche*, and I recommend both. You'll learn stories of the area from the carriage driver (be sure he is English-speaking before boarding), and this will enhance your walking tour. Be sure to pick up a tourist guide booklet at one of the information centers before your walking tour. A don't-miss is the ceremonial changing of the guard at The Citadel at 10 a.m. each day from the middle of June to the end of August.

You also will want to walk the Plains of Abraham in the National Battlefields Park. This is where the sleeping army of the Marquis de Montcalm was surprised and defeated in 20 minutes by the soldiers of British Gen. James Wolfe, who scaled the sheer cliffs, an almost-impossible feat, from the St. Lawrence River below.

Take a stroll from the Chateau on rue du Trésor to browse through the outdoor art gallery where local artists display and sell their works very much as they do on the Left Bank of the Seine in Paris.

Be sure to sample the elegant French cuisine at least once. Remember that no French meal is complete without dessert, and the desserts in Quebec are to die for. Many restaurants post their menus outside, so you may pick and choose to your heart's content. For lunch, you can want a lighter fare at a sidewalk café along the Grande Allée near the Parliament buildings.

Down from Chateau Frontenac is Lower Town in the Quartier Petit Champlain, where a group of renovated houses on different street levels contain all types of boutiques, indoor art galleries and outdoor cafés. A funicular railway connects Lower Town with Dufferin Terrace. For major shopping, downtown Quebec's huge, modern indoor complex is on St. Joseph Street.

The Quebec International Summer Festival begins the first Thursday in July and lasts 10 days. If you visit during this time, be sure to make hotel reservations well in advance. It is a grand celebration and attracts thousands of visitors.

BRITISH COLUMBIA

Across the continent on Vancouver Island in the Pacific Northwest lies the most British city in North America. Victoria, capital of British Columbia, is as English as Quebec is French. A visit to this city is appropriate if your grandchildren are 14 or older.

Standing guard over beautiful downtown Victoria as it curves softly about the Inner Harbour are the elaborate Parliament buildings.

The legislative gardens - English gardens, of course - contain playful fountains and dignified statues. It is quite relaxing.

Many movie companies select Victoria when filming a typical British city. They don't have to go abroad to film an English-looking countryside, Scottish moors or meadows. Victoria is considered Canada's safest city - one where you might allow your grandchildren the freedom to wander in and out of the shops in Trounce Alley without you.

Teenagers think the hand-woven woolens from Ireland and England are awesome. And few can resist the bittersweet chocolate, a favorite of the royal family, I'm told, from Rogers' Chocolate Shop.

Of course, high tea at the famous Fairmont Empress Hotel is a must for all. British teatime is usually 4 p.m., but you may opt for an earlier hour. Reservations are necessary and, for your young gentleman, a coat and tie. Many other restaurants in the city also require such attire. While at the Empress, don't fail to see the Miniature World on display. It is a colorful animation depicting scenes from history, Charles Dickens novels and fairy tales, to name a few.

Guided tours in the traditionally British red double-decker buses are available, as are the tally-ho horse-drawn carriages. Sports lovers will get into the British spirit with lawn bowling behind the Crystal Garden. Cricket is played at Beacon Hill Park. The numerous golf courses attest to the fact that golf is a favorite, and surf fishing here is excellent. You need a license for fishing, though, so check it out.

Craigdarroch Castle, built in the 1880s by a Scotsman, is not as old as those of Europe, but is interesting nonetheless.

North of Victoria is Butchart Gardens, a flower lover's delight no matter the time of year. If your grandchildren balk, leave them downtown to wander and take yourself to the gardens for a delightful day. Each season has more than 40 acres of spectacular color. You may pause for breakfast, lunch or dinner in either the Butchart Dining Room or the Blue Poppy. Live entertainment is offered in the evenings. From the middle of June until the middle of September, the gardens are illuminated at night and there are fireworks displays on Saturday nights in July and August.

Undoubtedly, your grandchildren will want some beach time while you're on Vancouver Island. Head southwest of Victoria about 25 miles to the corner of the island near Sooke, where the beaches are great and you will share them with friendly sea lions. You may even see whales. As you travel to and from the island on the ferry, be sure to have your binoculars handy to watch for whales and dolphins cavorting in the clear waters of Queen Charlotte Sound. They may not be British, but seeing them is a great way to bid farewell to a beautiful land.

MORE VISITS IN CANADA

Canada certainly has many more places you might want to take your grandchildren, depending on your and their inter ests. If you are of Scottish descent, you may want to visit St. Ann's, Nova Scotia, where the Gaelic language, bagpipe playing and Highland dancing are taught.

> 66 With or without your grandchildren, take the time to stroll about Government Street with its Victorian lampposts supporting bright baskets of multicolored flowers. 99

A visit to Stratford, Ontario, is the next best thing to visiting Shakespeare's birthplace in Stratford, England. A true replica on Canada's Avon River, it has a formal garden where every flower mentioned in a Shakespeare play blooms. The drama festival, lasting from early May to late September, presents evening performances on three different stages Tuesday through Sunday, with matinees on Wednesday, Saturday, Sunday and Friday.

From Winnipeg, Manitoba, you can take a Via Rail Tour north to Churchill, the polar bear capital of the world. This city on Hudson Bay lets you see these great bears in their natural habitat. It is a long train trip, leaving Winnipeg on Tuesday, Thursday or Saturday at 10 p.m. and arriving in Churchill two days later at about 8 in the morning. It travels through true wilderness areas and stops only in Dauphin, a Ukranian settlement, and The Pas, home of the World Championship Sled Dog Race. For information and reservations, write Via Rail Tours, 123 Main St., Winnipeg, MB, Canada R3C 2P8.

Your grandchild will be ecstatic over the rodeos, bronco busting, steer riding, chuckwagon racing and street dancing in Calgary. Be sure to indulge in the Stampede Breakfast, a meal of pancakes and syrup, spicy sausage, hot coffee and chilled juice, served by denim-clad hosts. These cowboys and cowgirls are everywhere you go - in parking lots, industrial areas, even in the Olympic Plaza.

CHAPTER 14

TRAVELING WITH A GRANDCHILD WHO HAS A DISABILITY

I f you have a handicapped grandchild - as I do - whom you want to take on a fun trip, ask yourself the following questions before mentioning it to anyone:

✔ Am I physically and emotionally able to assume this responsibility?

✔ Can I lift a wheelchair in and out of the car, fold and unfold it and place my grandchild in it with ease? Do I know how to lock and unlock the wheels? If it isn't working, can I make minor adjustments? Do I know how to change the batteries?

✔ In case of gastric-tube feeding, breathing exercises, diapering and other necessary routines, do I know how, where and when? Will it exhaust me to carry them out regularly?

✔ Am I able to lift my youngster in and out of the bathtub daily?

✔ If the child is hearing impaired, do I sign well enough to be understood?

✔ Do I know when to assist my visually challenged child and when to allow independence?

✔ Can I accept the sympathetic stares and whispered comments of passersby with a smile on my face without trying to explain or defend?

✔ Are my coping skills adequate for any type of emergency that might arise?

Assuming you have considered these questions long and hard and your responses are in the affirmative, your next step is to broach your plan with the parents. Ask for their honest opinions and advice. Do not - and I repeat, do not - feel hurt or insulted if they totally refuse the idea or subtly suggest that one of them accompany you. Remember: They not only are thinking of their child but also of you. Accept their suggestions and decisions with grace and appreciation.

You may not have thought of it, but taking one of the parents along could make the trip more pleasurable and relaxing for all. You could spend the same quality time with your grandchild and have help available if necessary.

You may not have thought of it, but taking one of the parents along could make the trip more pleasurable and relaxing for all. You could spend the same quality time with your grandchild and have help available if necessary. Such a trip also could give some valuable rest and relaxation to the parent.

If the word is go, your work has just begun. Planning, in this situation, is even more important than usual and needs to be started months in advance. You will need to move in with your children and grandchild for whatever period of time is necessary for you to learn everything necessary for the child's care.

After you, your young charge and his parents have chosen a destination, start your research. Most travel books provide good information, but they can't be counted on for accessibility issues.

Write to the chamber of commerce in the area you plan to visit, tell them your plans, explain your problem and ask for help. Someone there should be able to give you access information and likely will refer you to a disability organization in that city. The definition of accessibility may be in the eye of the beholder even though the 1990 passage of the Americans with Disabilities Act has done much to streamline public awareness. You might also want to consult AAA's new series of guides to barrier-free travel. These guides focus on specific destinations and accessibility concerns of those who are sight-impaired or hearing-impaired or who have mobility issues.

If you fly to your destination, don't hesitate to ask the airline about its policies toward disabled travelers such as:

✔ Will you be assisted in boarding?

✔ How about storing or transferring the wheelchair and its batteries (if any)?

✔ Can special dietary needs be met?

✔ How accessible are the bathrooms?

Find an airline that is aware of disability issues and is concerned for its passengers' comfort.

Do your own research. Be sure that your travel agent is aware of and understands the special concerns of your grandchild's disability.

When making hotel reservations, don't call the toll-free number. Call the hotel directly and make sure the reservationist understands your specific needs. Do as you did with the airlines: Ask questions. If you aren't satisfied with the answers, check with another hotel. The same advice goes for car rental agencies.

Your choice of a destination will be guided not only by your and your grandchild's interests, but also by the type and extent of his disability. If you want to keep traveling to a minimum, you may consider renting a condominium at a beach. This can be great fun if your grandchild is ambulatory. Gathering shells, jumping in and out of the waves and building sandcastles make for fun times. *Do not attempt to push a wheelchair through the sand. This could be dangerous.*

On the Outer Banks in North Carolina, there are several beaches with ramps and viewing platforms, but the beaches themselves are soft and not accessible to regular wheelchair traffic. Many beaches have surf chairs that will roll over the sand. Check this out before you go.

San Diego's Mission Beach in California has a cement boardwalk and accessible walkway to the hard-packed sand, where a regular wheelchair may be pushed with ease.

Mountain vacations in a hotel alongside a cool, rocky stream with good, hard-packed mountain trails leading up to waterfalls, coves, glens and wildflowers - you can't pick wildflowers in the National Parks - can be great for a child who is wheelchair-bound. The Great Smoky Mountains National Park is excellent for this.

A trip to our nation's capital is essential

if your grandchild is a history buff. The District of

Columbia's Metro system is

fully accessible.

A trip to our nation's capital is essential if your grandchild is a history buff. The District of Columbia's Metro system is fully accessible. All stations have an elevator to the platform, and a level surface from elevator to train. The Tourmobile has vans with lifts and lockdowns available with 24 hours advance notice. At The Smithsonian, the major spaces are accessible, guide dogs are allowed and visitors may request sign language interpreters or touch tours with advance notice.

Niagara Falls, Yellowstone National Park and Grand Canyon National Park are three of this nation's scenic wonders that are, for the most part, accessible for the disabled. Contact the parks before you go for any special tips.

There is much in larger cities that will interest any youngster. Problems can arise for those who are physically impaired when it comes to transportation to and from the airports. In New York City, most express buses do not have wheelchair lifts or lockdowns. Gray Line Air Shuttle (with 48 hours advance notice), has minibuses with lifts and Lockdowns and serves both LaGuardia and Newark airports and the major hotels. While more expensive than the express buses, it is considerably less than taxi cabs, which will store collapsible wheelchairs and assist the users.

Some Boston taxi companies have accessible taxis with ramps and tie-downs. Two-day notice is required. Call Boston Cabs or Checker cabs. In Los Angeles, MTA has buses with lifts and lockdowns running between Los Angeles International Airport and downtown hotels for a nominal fee, but finding transportation to other places of interest is difficult and expensive.

WALT DISNEY WORLD® RESORT

As I mentioned earlier, I normally don't consider visiting a theme park when traveling with my grandchildren. But there is an exception. There is no finer vacation spot to visit with a severely challenged grandchild than Walt Disney World® Resort in Orlando. It is such a happy place, filled with beauty, laughter, music and color. The staff is trained to treat exceptional children as the special little people they are. My little Sarah was given royal treatment.

When you make reservations, be sure to notify the hotel that you need wheelchair-accessible accommodations or have other special needs. When you get to the Walt Disney World® Resort entrance, you will receive a permit to park in the designated accessibility zone near the entrance. From then on, you will be assisted at every stop.

There will be no waiting lines for you. Cast members will escort you to exits and you will be whisked away to "magic land." Many attractions have special places for wheelchairs, so your grandchild can remain seated. Others require moving the child to a seat or to your lap. Cast members will help you and have the wheelchair waiting at the end of the ride.

You will find special, well-equipped feeding and changing stations at different places throughout the resort. And the characters who stroll about the resort will hurry forward to shake hands, pose for pictures or give autographs to your youngster.

I can't compliment the Walt Disney World® Resort cast highly enough for their helpfulness, their anticipation and their kindness and consideration when dealing with special children. This applies to the Magic Kingdom® Park, Epcot®, Disney-MGM Studios and Disney's Animal Kingdom®, Theme Park, and the hotels, not only within the resort, but also in the surrounding area. Regardless of where you stay and what you do, remember to pace your fun. You have a fragile charge. So go easy, relax, enjoy each other and have a wonderful time!

CHAPTER 15

WHAT TO DO ABOUT HOMESICKNESS AND OTHER PROBLEMS

No matter how well you plan your trip and how close you are with your grandchild, problems can appear. Darkness falls. The day is over. Tucked down in her hotel bed, Susie has visions of her home, her dog, her cat. Are they missing her? Did Mom remember to feed them? There is a big lump in her throat and it gets bigger and bigger. She can hardly breathe. Tears start.

What can you do? Just what comes naturally. Put your arms around her, cuddle her closely and talk soothingly. Get her to tell you how she feels and validate her feelings. Talking it out or getting involved in a new activity will go a long way toward alleviating the worst homesickness attack. Try puppet play or suggest she draw a picture of her family and pets.

If she won't talk, a call home will help a lot. There's no rule that says there shouldn't be frequent calls back home if desired. If you get on the phone after she talks, speak glowingly of your plans for the next day. Hearing this and anticipating the fun of tomorrow may deter any more problems at that time. In extreme cases when nothing works, ask her if she wants to go home tomorrow. She probably will say yes, but by morning may have changed her mind. If she still wants to go home, take her. She just wasn't ready.

Older children may miss their friends as much as family and pets. Here, too, telephone calls can solve a lot. Most kids like to share their activities with a friend. Grandparents might want to disappear for a little while to allow some telephone conversation privacy.

If you are traveling with one grandchild, your chances for a relatively peaceful time are greater. The dynamics are different. It is almost like you are best friends rather than grandparent-grandchild. You are sharing special things and laughing over silly little things that happened during the day.

It is almost like you are best friends

rather than grandparent-grandchild.

You are sharing special things and laughing over

silly little things that happened during the day.

Unless you are the exception and have absolute angels for grandkids, there will be some spats and probably tears, maybe even a tantrum along the way. Just relax and keep your cool. You've handled all this before. Nothing has changed that much since this youngster's parent was your child. Let her know that you know how she feels, but that sometimes it is impossible - too dangerous, too expensive or whatever - to permit you to grant her every wish. The less you say the better. Listen if she wants to talk. Cut off the conversation if she wants to beg. Remind her that your "no" means just that. Say it and hush.

When she begins to cool down, you may suggest a new activity. A new adventure will make her forget her anger. Physical activity usually helps abate whining, an irritant to most grandparents. A romp in the park, a hike around the hotel grounds or a swim in the pool expends some of that pent-up energy and creates a more pleasant traveling experience.

If your grandchild becomes fearful of an activity such as horseback riding or water rafting, even if it's something she said she wanted desperately to do, let her know that no plans are etched in stone. It is OK to back out. If she wants to watch, fine. Chances are she will want to participate later. Never force a child into an activity against her will.

There may be a reason - if only in your grandchild's mind - to fear a place. Perhaps you just arrived in California and someone mentioned earthquakes. She suddenly wants to go home. Sit down with her and explain that it is very doubtful there will be an earthquake, but if there should be, you are her grandparent, you love her very much and you will take care of her. That simple and true statement can give her the security she needs.

Adolescents present a different problem. They become bored easily and with boredom may come complaining or silent pouting. What do you do? Think back to when you were planning the trip. Remember what really interested him. Tell him you wished you could find a place to do that activity. Thumb through the yellow pages. It won't be long before he'll be trying to help you.

The real problem is that this may not happen when you are in your hotel room. You may be in the car during a long day or on an airplane. After a brief silence, you might ask a thought-provoking question - one that requires a considered opinion and an explanation. This can be the beginning of real communication and can dispel the boredom.

Rainy days at the beach - or anywhere else for that matter - can test any grandparent's creativity. This may be a good time to pull out the new travel game you were saving for such an emergency. Shopping for souvenirs, visiting a mall or spending time in a toy store can make the time pass more quickly. Movies are great, as are museums. It might pay to drive some distance for either. Who knows? By the time you are out, the sun may be shining.

Traveling with children always requires patience and flexibility. Be aware of their feelings. If they tend to be homesick or fearful, acknowledge these feelings. That will help the child cope with them. As much as possible, stick to a familiar schedule. Always encourage your grandchildren to talk about anything that bothers them. Show how much you value and respect them. Most of all, use your good common sense and let your love and joy in your grandchildren show through.

IN CONCLUSION

The vacations discussed in this book have only scratched the surface of the travel possibilities with your grandchildren. With any luck it has stimulated your imagination and interest and will serve as a guide in planning your own wonderful trips. Remember that if your budget is limited, your grandchildren are young or you feel a little insecure, *stay close to home.*

Always try to find places to visit that are friendly to children. And no matter how many children you take, how much or how little money you spend, keep the faith. You are in for the adventure of a lifetime.

So here's to all you travel-loving grandparents who want to share experiences and make lifelong memories with your grandchildren. I bid you *Bon voyage!*

Virginia Smith Spurlock

 # The One That Does It All

For years, people have turned to AAA for their emergency road service needs. But AAA is more than just towing. Access to AAA's travel services can give you the world. Its financial services can help you pay for it. And AAA insurance can give you the peace of mind to enjoy the ride.

Plus AAA gives you exclusive Show Your Card & Save® offers and much more.

Discover the ways AAA can simplify your life. Call 800-JOINAAA, visit aaa.com or stop by your nearest AAA office today to find out about the specific products and services AAA offers.

NOTES

NOTES

NOTES

NOTES